RECALIBRATE FOR LIFE 2.0

Transition Stories for Business Leaders

by

Susan K. Spaulding

RECALIBRATE FOR LIFE 2.0:

CONTENTS

RECALIBRATE FOR LIFE 2.0:

THE RECALIBRATION OPPORTUNITY

It wasn't in my business plan to be a consulting resource for senior leaders and business owners moving toward retirement. I'm a business consultant–and Boomer–with my own questions about what I now call Life 2.0.

I happened into this focus nearly by accident.

In my work I am continuously observing human behavior and the combination of rational and emotional forces that push us to the decisions we make.

And, after having a series of "what's going on here...moments, I realized there were stories that needed to be shared.

The Journey to Life 2.0 Research

After selling my own market research company to become a partner in a larger business, I found the 80-hour-a-week work schedule and life lived on airplanes had gotten old. So I left the partnership for more flexibility and peace. But it didn't take long to know I missed the world of business, helping companies develop market-driven business strategies.

This start-up generated the opportunity for meetings with business colleagues. And during those meetings, I became part of a series of interesting–and surprising– conversations.

Most often, the conversation would begin with curiosity about my exit from the partnership and the high-flying but intense world it had provided me. What led me to the decision to leave? And more importantly, how did I decide what would be next?

It didn't take many rounds of coffee and lunches to understand the very successful executives and business owners I was meeting with were not wondering about my exit plans. They were wondering about theirs. Some were at the top of their respective careers and nearing age-driven considerations about retirement. Others were feeling the inner push of simple readiness for a change. They wanted more flexibility, perhaps, or the chance to pursue passions or interests or even business ideas that the demands of life had postponed.

But how were they to decide when to make a change? And when that time came, how would they know what to change to?

They seemed to be asking, "What should I be now that I'm grown up?" And as importantly, "How will I decide?"

The Arrival of the Silver Tsunami

After a series of these conversations, the years I'd spent as a consumer behaviorist involved in marketing research took over. I was aware of the cultural setting driving these questions, a phenomenon called by some The Silver Tsunami. Roughly 10,000 Baby Boomers will turn 65 every day for the next 19 years.

I began to look at the studies of these potential retirees.

For instance, the Transamerica Center for Retirement Studies reported: "For most Baby Boomer workers, retirement is no longer a point in time in which one immediately stops working. Sixty-eight percent of Baby Boomer workers envision a phased transition into retirement during which they will either continue working, reduce hours with more leisure time to enjoy life, or work in a different capacity that is less demanding and/or brings greater personal satisfaction. Only 21 percent expect to immediately stop working when they retire, and 12 percent are 'not sure.'"

A curiosity about all these options was common among the business leaders who spoke with me.

Options for Senior Leaders

Quandaries about retirement were common. But I soon began to see three specific challenges as leaders discussed their futures.

First, many leaders and business owners didn't see retirement as a welcome escape from workplace captivity. Rather than drudgery and oppression, their career experiences were often rich and fulfilling; indeed, a good fit. Thoughts about making changes came from an interest in more flexible ways to do what they loved or perhaps the opportunity to explore equally fulfilling other options. There was little talk about a life spent 24/7 hitting a golf ball.

Second, these leaders could point to few models that could show them the way to a revised life plan. Preceding generations often didn't enjoy the longevity or good health so characteristic of the Boomers; many lacked resources to think in terms of new ventures. So, Life 2.0 pathways were yet to be created.

Third, I found a consistent awkwardness at the mention of the "R" word. It wasn't the question of a life change that proved uncomfortable; rather, it was the retiree designation with all the baggage attached to the word. One leader said, "Tell people you're retired, and they think of a decrepit, useless codger. They tend to ask, 'So, what did you used to do?' And I hear, 'What did you do when you were worth something?'"

Because this is true, many of us are struggling with a good name for what's next after a major career investment. I've heard it renamed "Re-firement." And, what about "Fabulescence" –a take on this better version of adolescence we can enjoy as we venture into uncharted territory. And I've thought of "Free-tirement," as a way to describe the freedom we now might enjoy to do what we want, whenever we want, however we want.

The struggle for a naming convention for this life period only highlights what I heard again and again. Senior executives and business owners have unique challenges as we face these re-invention years, and we aren't sure how to go about it.

An Experiment

Again, my history in marketing kicked in. Did my years thinking with companies about branding have relevance here? Branding is, after all, a process of looking at a company or a product's identity and often clarifying and sometimes re-defining that identity to meet new challenges.

What would happen if I used a re-branding process to help senior leaders recalibrate their identities?

The answer became an experimental workshop for which I brought together a group of executives to explore the rational and emotional underpinnings of exiting a career. And together we stepped into the discovery process of designing a way forward.

Lessons from the Workshop

The conversation was lively; the dialogue was open. And from the time I spent with those execs, two learnings became quickly clear:

First, redesigning life wouldn't be an event; it would be a process. Though we went through exploratory exercises and attempted action planning, it was clear answers to their life re-design questions weren't going to come by applying some neatly packaged formula. We left with small "next steps" for a journey, not a once-and-done list of answers.

Second, there was great power in community. By the very nature of the work of leadership, senior leaders have to keep much of their thinking close to the vest. Our level of responsibility for others demands discretion and careful disclosure to wisely selected thought partners. So, several in that workshop commented on the relief they felt at being in the presence of peers–others who, like them, lacked clear answers, but could openly voice their uncertainty without fearing repercussions. For some the sense of not being alone in this quest offered great encouragement.

The feedback from these executives became the incentive for

this project. It seemed clear there'd be a contribution by interviewing senior leaders who were coming at retirement from various views, with varying strategies, and with varying outcomes.

We'd help each other in this life re-creation process.

The Stories Ahead

You'll find ahead conversations with fourteen executives, largely C-level corporate leaders, or business owners who chose to disclose with honesty and with their insights, ideas and strategies as they carved out a path to a life change.

Here are the fellow leaders you'll be getting to know and learning from:

- Karl Eberle was a senior leader in manufacturing of an iconic international brand; he's now doing a variation on that work as a consultant.
- Siobhan McLauglin Lesley and Larry Bigus each is moving to leadership in the not-for-profit world from highly successful careers; Siobhan in advertising and Larry as an attorney.
- Steve Rutledge leads his own marketing consulting business and does this by adapting to market conditions and continuously exploring ways to bring value to others.
- Connie Swartz and Barry Morris have both leveraged their talents as entrepreneurs into new ventures, while Barbara Allan and her spouse Bob Allan are finding ways to adapt their current business partnership to fit their changing interests and priorities.
- Cameron Bishop ran a highly diversified portfolio of media properties and is now a partner in a management consulting firm where he focuses on helping companies build value.
- Rob Givens and Peter Nussbaum each retired from high-level leadership positions; Rob as a CEO in the financial services industry and Peter as one of the top lawyers in the country and a senior partner in a well-respected law firm. Now both are exploring interests that had to be shelved in the intensity of their first careers and are finding ways to invest in their communities.

- Bill Fialka, a former CEO, found that through a trial run having his own business wasn't a fit and now works productively as part of another organization.
- Delphyne Lomax is co-leader of a marketing services firm; Pamela Kelley was an executive in the entertainment industry. Both are finding ways to create new opportunities for themselves and others, Delphyne in the world of paid work and Pamela in a venture to develop a not-for-profit with a political focus.
- Dennis Dunlap served as CEO of the largest marketing association and is now leveraging that platform to look for global opportunities for growth.

I think you'll find, as I did, that the power of their stories is less in where they ended than in how they got there. In each case, a way of thinking about life and work was applied to this new question of 'What's next?' Each approached his or her re-invention or re-focus with a particular mindset or approach to problem-solving that helped design their path.

Karl Eberle, for example, has been a "fixer" his entire career. First he fixed manufacturing issues; now he proposes fixes for companies trying to find their way to better leadership, processes and measures. And in between, he finds joy in concrete fixes to home repairs for his family and others.

In contrast, Rob Givens led as a CEO, but a big driver behind his interest in the world of credit unions was entangled in the possibility of community development. Now, in volunteer roles, he serves on boards and in mentoring roles that directly impact communities and their growth.

The setting for these two may have shifted, but their approaches and drivers didn't.

As you hear from the leaders who share their stories, be on the alert for approaches that feel like a fit for you.

Looking for Applications

You'll find at the end of each chapter, my take on lessons from the interviewees' experiences. These takeaways may help you find useful learning from what others found helpful.

You'll also find questions to consider. Some may intrigue you; others won't. But these interviews aren't intended to be an end in themselves. They're here to help you craft your own story as you recreate an identity for the next stage of your life.

So now, come join in the dialogue with fourteen of your colleagues as we talk about generating Life 2.0.

RECALIBRATE FOR LIFE 2.0:

TRANSITION STORIES FOR BUSINESS LEADERS

THE STORIES

LIFE 2.0

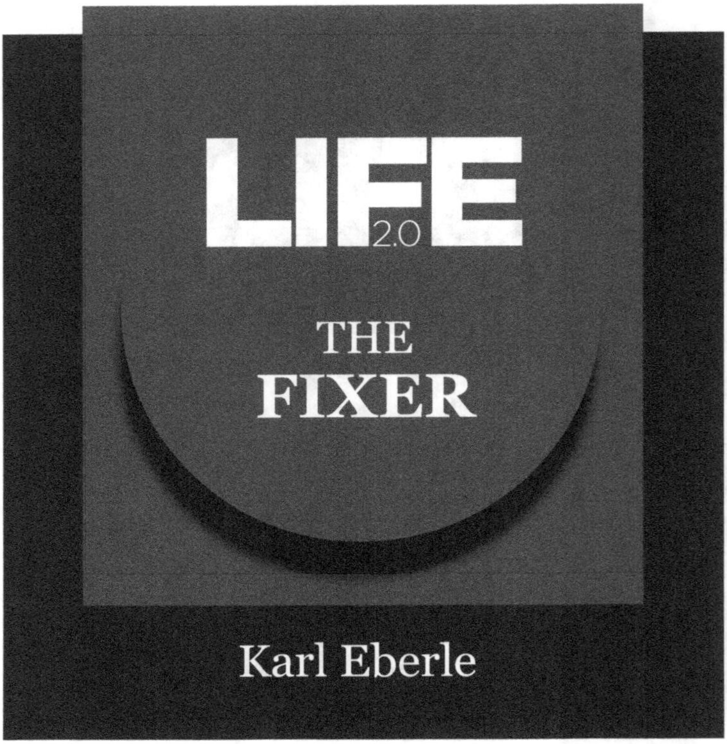

Any of us in senior leadership have done our share of training events that test us for our leadership style. We've learned our Myers-Briggs profile, and our "personality color type" and all the rest.

Some of this work offered useful insights; other experiences were just entertaining. But the reason all these diagnostics retain their popularity is this: we don't come at life the same way. The sooner we get clear on our own uniqueness, the more empowered we are to efficiently use that uniqueness to our advantage.

I found this often as senior leaders told me about their approaches to next-life planning.

Some of these leaders are thorough analysts who develop great solutions through thoughtful research and calculated initiatives.

Then there are others, like Karl Eberle, who you are about to meet.

Karl doesn't complicate matters when there are next steps to be taken. He gets just enough information to frame the problem and moves ahead to solve it. Indeed, I found the theme of "fixing" and "solving" coming up repeatedly in our conversation. Because of his life approach, I think he offers a way to move forward that will fit well for those of us who prefer to analyze less, do more and see what happens.

"While you were still at Harley-Davidson, had you given much thought to a plan for retirement?"

"Actually, I did a lot of thinking about what could be next. I met with people who had retired and asked them how they chose to do what they were doing. I learned this: either they got into something very close to what they did when they worked corporate or they were going a direction one hundred and eighty degrees in the opposite direction. There wasn't much middle ground."

"Interesting. So what guidance did that offer you as you looked at your own future?"

"It seemed to me that if I went the route of doing what I knew –manufacturing–that consulting would be a good format. Now, I wouldn't have started with the idea of consulting; I hated consultants when I worked at Harley."

"What changed for you?"

"It occurred to me that I could do consulting differently–be myself in it and treat customers the way I wish I had been treated by consultants. So I decided, 'What the hell? I'll give it a try!'

"I started by billing myself as a manufacturing consultant. My years with Harley, John Deere and others set me up well for that tagline. Now my work in companies usually starts with manufacturing, but I wind up spending probably half my time consulting on leadership issues. I'm either looking at incompetence or misplaced people or misguided strategy for today's situation. Actually, I never dreamed I'd spend that much time on the leadership part, the people part, but that's often where the hold-ups are."

"So, are you finding your fit in companies much like Deere and Harley?"

"Actually, I'm working with a company right now that makes iron on 'heat transfers' and screen prints for garments/T-shirts –probably producing a hundred thousand of these a day. Pretty different from Harley! But I'm finding it doesn't matter what the business is. If you don't have the right processes and metrics and leadership in place, you're screwed. So, that's where I spend my time."

"You've been at this about three years. How much do you work?"

"The first year I probably worked ten days a month. Last year it grew to 18 days a month, but I quickly saw that was too much. So, now I'm working six to eight days. After these experiences, I think about ten days a month felt pretty close to right."

"Now that I understand how much work is comfortable, I'm out to pick up another client. I want to always have at least two underway at any one time, so if one folds I'm not left high and dry. I'd like to keep at this business for the next ten years or so."

"Let's back up to the beginning. How did you find your first client?"

"I got interested in private equity firms as potential clients because they often need help cleaning up operations before companies are ready for sale. They are involved with multiple businesses and actively look for consultants for turnarounds and operational improvements. Because of my years in manufacturing, I knew that part of the business well. I had high-level qualifications from the time at Harley and having the LEAN manufacturing system under my belt. I figured I'd be a fit."

"The question was how to connect with these private equity firms. So I hired an executive recruiter to identify a target list and pre-qualify organizations I could approach. The recruiter also introduced me to business leaders in my area who had connections with firms I might like to pursue."

"And I went to New York and Chicago to do some cold calling on firms. I hated it - felt too much like selling pots and pans. But I did make some connections and got two good engagements – one working on a labor dispute in Pennsylvania, and another in manufacturing in a plant in Missouri."

"The first was the hardest. I hadn't done this before, so going into that first company was a little scary. Fear of the unknown, probably. I wanted to bring value and wasn't sure yet how much I could. But then I remembered all the consultants I'd worked with during my corporate years, and told myself, 'S***! I can do as much as they can do!' That thought was enough to get me started. And once I was underway with the work and got involved with the people, it turned out to be better than I thought. I was surprised."

"Since then, what have you learned about choosing which companies are a fit for you?"

"I'm not sure I could make a list of the qualities I want in customers. But this I knew: I want to work with ones who want me there. I don't need to put up with a lot of resistance to my ideas, and if there is resistance, I don't believe I'd be helping them anyway. Once I understood that, making customer connections came easier."

"But I have to work at what's harder for me: continuing to develop relationships that build enough trust that people will ask me to help them. And I need to be getting out and growing these relationships while I'm working with customers; otherwise when one job ends, there won't be another to replace it."

"Sort of continually marketing. It's the other side of the freedom of self-employment."

"That's it. I've helped eight businesses in the three years since leaving Harley, so I've more than gotten my feet wet. I just need to keep at those connections so the work I want to do is there for me when I'm ready. That's new, but I'm learning."

"You like the flexibility of this life. That seems clear."

"So true. When I had a job with global responsibilities, I was gone from home 80% of the time. I remember seeing a picture one of my kids had drawn of our family; Dad had a cell phone hanging off his ear, probably because that's how she almost always saw me. Now I've got time for my kids and friends. Lots of options are open I didn't have before."

"For instance, like the time my daughter had a leak in the bathroom above her kitchen ceiling and a plumber told her it would take several thousand dollars to fix it. So I jumped in, tore out the shower, and plumbed that bathroom. It took five days and a lot of work. I didn't retire to spend all my time doing home repairs, of course, but being able to do something to solve that problem for her felt really good."

"And more flexibility to pursue recreation, too?"

"Absolutely. The first year I was retired, an old friend and I went on a six-week motorcycle trip to the Pacific Northwest. We did all the national parks from here to the west coast. Last year we went to Maine in the fall. I go salmon fishing in Alaska regularly, too."

"We have an apartment in Spain where we go a couple of weeks a year. And I've been able to do some international travel with my daughter–Machu Picchu was our last trip. Who does all that when you're running a major operation?"

"I'm in good shape financially, so the consulting money (I call it my "Monopoly money") lets me make some of these choices, plus help some people I might not be able to otherwise. Or at least able to help them as generously."

"Great positives in this new life. What do you miss about the corporate life?"

"Consistent professional contact, for sure. I liked the constant interaction with people who interested me."

"However, in this work I'm doing now, I'm pretty much focused on the CEO in smaller companies or the General Manager in larger ones. So these are enjoyable peer relationships where I am fairly sure something's going to change in the company because I worked with them. That helps with the issue of missing the team work environment I enjoyed a lot."

"I'll admit I miss having support people I can count on to get things done. (I still don't know how to build an Excel spreadsheet.) And there are also the executive perks. The paid-for- trips to motorcycle rallies, for instance, and then there's access to the jet..."

"But I'll say this; consulting the way I am doing it is fun because people seek you out when they've identified they have a problem to be solved; otherwise, they'd have no reason to call you. They want your help, and if you choose the jobs well, you have the solutions they are looking for."

"It's like the manufacturer I worked with in New Jersey. The company owner always picks me up at the airport and drops me off. After my third visit, when he dropped me off, I went to shake hands and instead he gave me a big hug. He said, 'We are going to make it!"

"I thought, 'I hardly know you, and here you are embracing me.' But it was gratitude; I knew it. Early in my work with him, I suggested starting a production meeting for his staff, so I'd call in every day to the meeting, not to lead it, but to listen. But during the meeting, this client would ask me, 'What do you think we should do about this or that?' and I'd weigh in. And then I'd hear him say to others in the meeting, 'Okay, we've got our marching orders now. We've got to do this stuff.' It was clear to me my input was making a difference. I could live for a long time on results like that."

"Now, three years and eight clients into this world of consulting, what would you say you brought from your career that helps others the most?"

"I know it makes a difference that my larger company experience gives me perspective they might not have. I tell clients, 'You can't know what you don't know, and some of what I see is just because I've been with larger companies where it's possible to get a broader view. Let's put that to work for you."

"And I seem to have good sense about how to introduce change at a rate they can deal with, so the change sticks. I've seen new systems brought into companies that completely fail because the implementation was pushed through too quickly."

"And I've found I may be unique in that I can relate to people at all levels. I enjoy the employees on the manufacturing floor as much as I do the company presidents. And I can help with both strategy and tactics–that seems to make a big difference."

"It sounds like you repurposed great capacity from your old life that drives lots of levels of problem-solving. What would you say now to others who are where you were three years ago – looking at retiring and at changes ahead?"

"Don't throw out your past too quickly. You may be sick of what you did, but that doesn't mean there isn't a way you can use it differently that's more comfortable. You've spent your life learning; in all that time you've surely gotten something that would be applicable to others. Most of us in bigger companies don't have a clear sense of what our knowledge and experience is worth."

Takeaways to Consider

- Remain open to using your knowledge and skills in new ways.
- Choose clients and partners ready to listen and question.
- Place a priority on partnering with those you like and trust.
- Engage with experts to expand your knowledge and jump-start your thinking.

Questions to Ask Yourself

- From my past, what would I like to recalibrate and leverage in the future?
- What is my uniqueness?
- Do I have relationships that already know and trust me?

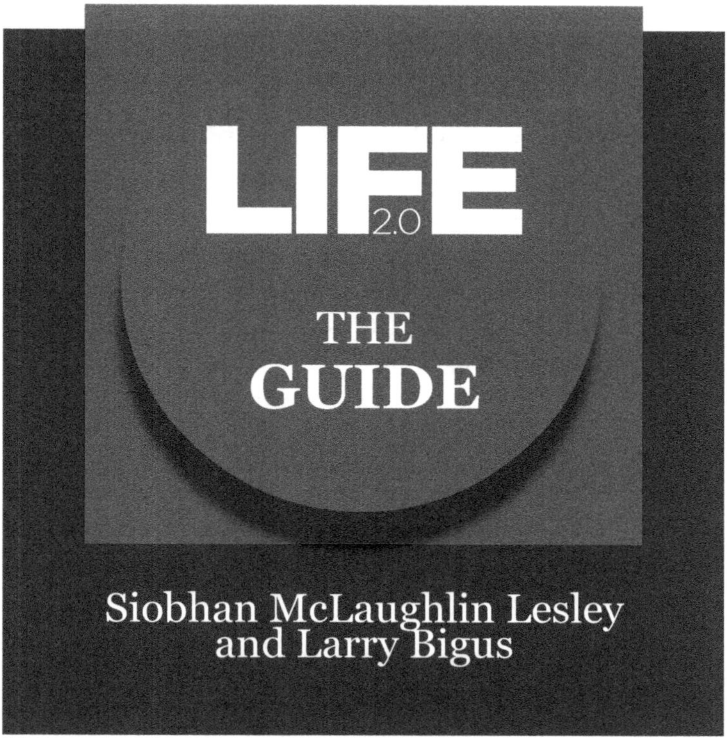

A book title that surfaced ten years ago seemed to capture the quiet desire of some of those I spoke with about life after their current careers. The book was called *From Success to Significance.*

For some who've accomplished what they dreamed of in their work lives, simply doing more of the same holds little interest. Other motivations, like making a difference or creating a lasting contribution became more important guides for their energy investment in the years after retirement.

Senior business leaders Siobhan McLaughlin Lesley and Larry Bigus would, on the surface, seem to have little in common professionally. Siobhan is an advertising executive; Larry a deeply seasoned attorney specializing in commercial law with an emphasis in recent years in bankruptcy law.

But they share a sense of commitment to generating societal improvement and are making choices in retirement that allow them to reframe their work lives around this commitment.

Conversation with Siobhan McLaughlin Lesley

This top-of-her-game advertising and marketing professional was ready for a change. She'd managed advertising for franchises like Pizza Hut and had been responsible for prestigious accounts like Hallmark. She'd led Client Services, and then served as president and COO of an agency. There weren't many mountains left to climb.

However, during these years in advertising, Siobhan had also followed her passions for families and the arts into volunteer positions with more than ten organizations from the Ballet to Goodwill. At last she reached a point in her work life where she found herself thinking more and more about investing in community service.

"It sounds like your move into the not-for-profit world started with unrest."

"It did. I had a conversation with a marketing director for the United Way who told me about the point in his life when he decided to shift from working for money to working for meaning. That tag line stuck with me."

"For the longest time I convinced myself that to help others, being a good manager, being a good corporate citizen, setting a good example and volunteering on the side was enough. I was helping others."

"And when as part of my job, I'd help our client Dairy Queen pull off a treat day that supported the Children's Miracle Network, it seemed reasonable to tell myself I was fulfilling my desire to help kids. But I knew I was also working on increasing Dairy Queen's sales. And even though I believe Dairy Queen is very supportive to the communities they serve, for me that involvement on my part was too far from the action. I needed more."

"I got to the point where I'd wake up every morning and think about my non-profit board activities, or a project I was doing for this group or that, and not so much about the work for which I was getting paid. I began to tell myself, 'I'm a marketer, a developer, a communicator and at the end of the day, a sales person. Isn't there a way I could combine what I'm doing in the community with what I know how to do? Can't I do what I know for meaning, instead of just for money?"

"So did you jump right into the non-profit world?"

"Not initially. I did move to a different company in a position that allowed me to come and go as I pleased, and whose CEO blessed my involvement in various volunteer efforts. So I could be even more active with the groups I was helping."

"But it still wasn't enough. So after alerting my CEO about my intentions, I began sending out feelers at Board meetings, cocktail parties and networking events that I was looking for a place to give more aggressively in the not-for-profit world."

"My passions are clear: women, children, the arts. So that served as a filter as I talked with people. And I wanted to own the responsibility, not just provide recommendations to decision-makers who'd make things happen."

"Did it take long to find options?"

"Not really. My networking paid off, and before long a recruiter with an intriguing option contacted me. A Legoland and aquarium were slated to open at a downtown shopping area; I was approached to consider taking on the management of it."

"At first I thought, 'Gosh. That's a great asset for my city, and the location is part of our cultural tapestry. Plus, Legoland and an aquarium fit with my vision to help kids."

"But finding out more helped change my mind. Just before I was to fly to London for the final interview, I learned the hiring company had a plan I hadn't considered. 'You can probably get this venture to be successful in three to five years,' I was told.

'Then we'll move you up to Singapore or Australia to head a larger entity."

"The possibility of a move stopped me up short. My intention was a contribution to the city where I lived. But I had to have an attractive offer that required a move in order to understand how wed I am to this community."

"What next?"

"I spoke with a firm that provided fund-raising and development services to nonprofits. It looked like a fit. I figured that working with this organization, I could help lots of nonprofits, and still have my foot in the world of business I know so well."

"But with more consideration, the flaw in this position became clear. I wanted to be the decision maker. As a development professional I could write a great plan with stellar recommendations, but the client had to decide whether or not to accept it. It mattered to me that I was in the driver's seat, making decisions that in the end were mine to implement."

"It sounds like each of these options offered you chances to better understand your own priorities. How did you use this knowledge to keep moving forward?"

"Well, not long after, two different possibilities came to my attention. One involved directing a well-known support facility for families seeking medical attention for their critically-ill children. And besides the fit to my passion for children, the scope of work included managing four locations with 186 units, so the responsibility challenged me. And funding comes from local fundraising, so the buck would stop with me-literally-to make the enterprise successful."

"The other opportunity involved a key position in the city public library system. Along with administrative work, the position would draw richly on my background in marketing and community relations."

"How did your years in business appear to fit you for these roles?

"I think having business experience would allow me to move quickly growing these organizations, perhaps more quickly than if my professional background had been in a social services setting.

"But I know I'd have to exercise caution to move too quickly. The not-for-profit world has different forces at play, and the pace of change is sometimes slower. But to my mind, each of these causes, or causes like them, would be worth investing in until I do see lasting change."

"Did all those years as a volunteer on boards and advisory committees also help you in deciding to be considered for these positions?"

"Actually, to my mind, those years of experience working in volunteer roles will serve me well as I lead teams of volunteers. And my volunteer roles have helped me grow a broad network that will be useful for the challenges ahead."

A Conversation with Larry Bigus

Larry Bigus currently serves as executive director of an organization that provides support to low-income families through the winter months. But he came to this work following an unlikely path after a rich career practicing law, first with his father and later with large law firms.

"With your work history, many would have expected you'd finish a great law career, and perhaps just move on to retirement."

"In 2013 I had closed out a great year. I led a great team of great people working on a large and lucrative case. But in 2014, our company merged with another, larger one. As a result of complexities of the merger, I found I wasn't enjoying the work anymore; it was drudgery to get up and go to work."

"I had originally planned to retire in 2017, but the circumstances generated by the merger and other events beyond my control prompted me to jointly with the firm make the decision to leave."

"What were you thinking then about options?"

"I considered going to another law firm and explored that by talking to a number of smaller firms. But thinking it through, I could see that in a move I'd have to build back up, which would likely require a process of a couple of years. Since I'd already decided I wasn't going to stay in practice another 5-10 years, doing that work of rebuilding didn't seem reasonable.

"I also considered going corporate with an in-house legal department. But I wasn't interested in starting at the bottom, and positions at the top are few and far between with the right corporations.

"In time I began asking, 'What else could I do? Where might my skill set fit?'"

"Where did you look for answers to these questions?"

"Practicing law was an obvious skill set. And sailing is one of my passions, but not only would that not earn much money, I never wanted to turn a hobby into a profession.

"So, I started working on a rough resume, asking myself, 'What have I done in my life? And I began showing it to others, to professional friends and social friends whose opinions I value and asking them what they saw in the resume."

"They told me I had the ability to get along with people and motivate people. And they pointed to the fact that over the years I'd done a tremendous amount of volunteer work and served in leadership roles in volunteer organizations. From the time I was a teenager in youth groups to the time I was looking to make a move, I had nearly always been involved in leadership roles in some civic–or sometimes multiple–civic organizations. I've seen good and bad. I've run fundraisers. The not-for-profit world was not new territory for me."

"Some things began to clarify. I knew I wanted to do something to help people. That was actually a lot of my motivation for going into law in the first place. And I always wanted something I could be successful doing. In time, I realized I might be successful at running a charity. From my volunteer experience, I knew how they worked, and that I could deal well with the people involved."

"How did you proceed? Did you look at a lot of options, or did the one you chose seek you out?"

"I looked at options. First I looked at bigger charities, but it became obvious they wanted someone who had been a professional at a charity; a bias toward a lateral move rather than someone from the outside coming in. So it seemed reasonable to look for a smaller organization, and that was fine with me. I started looking through various resources and found the charity I now lead."

"What seems to be working in your re-invented role?"

"First, it's a great cause; we help low-income families get through the winter holiday season. And we have an absolutely wonderful group of volunteers. They're the heart and soul of the organization, passionate about helping their neighbors and willing to give time and resources to do so. And the work environment is very collegial."

"Where would you say major learning is taking place for you?"

"I knew pretty well what an executive director did before I took the job. So the learning curve for me was more becoming familiar with this organization."

"In my volunteer days, I saw great executive directors and horrible ones. And those experiences taught me the importance of a leader first learning the people and personalities before pushing for major change. And figuring out the strengths and challenges of the organization. And letting people know who you are, what you're about, how they're going to work with you. Then finding out the history of the organization and the cycle of events during the year. And what's worked and what hasn't."

"Some people who work in the not-for-profit sector tell me the pace is slower than many other business settings, and a wise leader will adjust.

It sounds like with this listen-and-learn-first strategy, you did just that. What would you like to accomplish in your time with the organization?"

"It's already a strong organization; I'd like to help make it even stronger by increasing the volunteer base to include more young people. And I'd like to see the financial base and visibility increase so we can help more and more low-income families."

"I'd say your plate is pretty full. Do you still have time to sail?"

"I do, and we consistently travel to see our children. But that can happen because when I took the job, I told the board that visiting our three children, none of whom live in the same state, was very important to me, and they agreed to that. So now when I visit my daughter who is in med school, I may work for four or five hours while she is studying. Electronics allow for that. And in January, when the holidays are over, our work pace is slowed so my wife and I do more traveling for pleasure."

"You speak of your wife. What part did she play in this transition?"

"When I originally went home and told her I was thinking of retiring, she said, 'You are not. I don't care how much money you make, and I don't really care what you do, but you are going to find something.' And she was right. I'm not a person who can sit around and do nothing, and going sailing seven days a week couldn't be the answer because then it's no longer a hobby."

"But my wife has her own business and is a bit of a workaholic herself, so having me committed to something helped us both. And she's also very charitable. So she supported this solution – working in a non-profit – because besides my being happy there, we are doing good and helping people. She has no issue with taking a lower income to work in a civic organization."

"That's important. The choices each of you make influences the other, and this new direction had a lot of implications for the two of you."

"It was important. If I had gone home and said I was taking a job with a significantly lower income and she had said, 'But I want a new car and a bigger home,' then I'd have a challenge on my hands. What I'm doing now wouldn't work with a spouse who wasn't supportive."

"This change seems to be working well. What advice would you offer others who are thinking about a change?"

"I'd say get started. Otherwise you'll find yourself ten years down the road and unhappy, and you'll feel pushed into a change. But you don't start the process and a week later make the change. I began the process somewhat in 2014 and I walked into my new job in June of 2015; it took a year."

"And no one else is going to do this for you; opportunity isn't going to fall into your lap. You have to create the opportunity, and that takes time. And it will take work. Self-reflection is hard. You'll find you see not just your positive qualities, but things you need to work on as well. But if you just get started, you have a much better shot at landing in a great fit."

Takeaways to Consider

- Discomfort can lead to breakthrough thinking.
- Consider what meaning you want as an indicator about what type of work to pursue.
- Planning and exploration help guide the skill shifts necessary to move from the profit to non-profit world.
- Patience is a virtue as you learn a new environment and build your team.

Questions to Ask Yourself

- Is non-profit leadership a change I would want?
- Do I have a charitable interest where my skills are needed?
- What are some skills or knowledge I might need to add or amplify for the non-profit world?
- What are the ways I can engage a new team before imparting sweeping change?

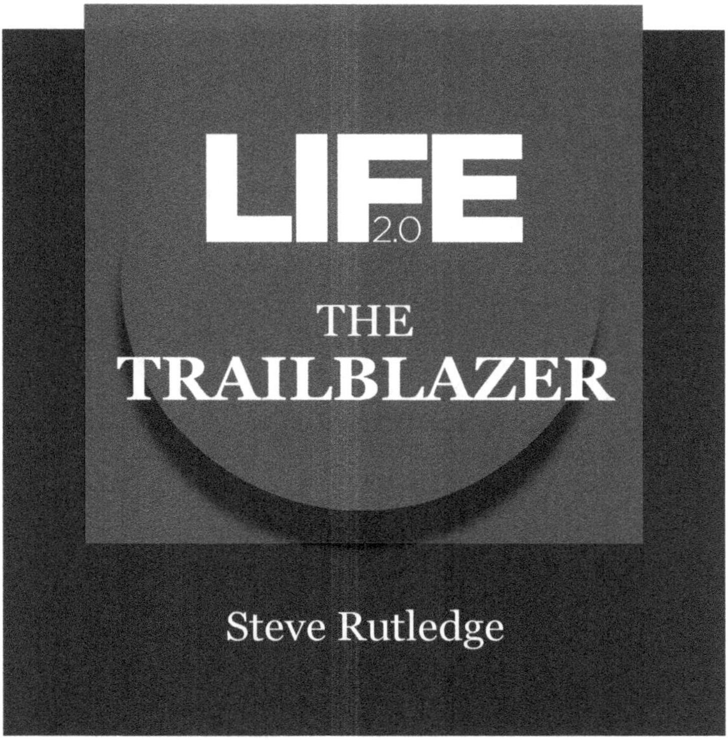

The world of marketing is based on connecting products and services with the people who will buy them. And here's the synopsis of Marketing 101: people only buy products or services that appear to offer more value to them than does hanging onto their money. Great marketing isn't first about a product; it starts with a customer's wants and needs.

When we get ready to transition to a new phase of contribution, aka retirement, it's important to be looking at what we want and need. (Thus the origin of all those "what would you love to do" questions we are often asked.)

But if what we want to do involves others-and all work does-we have to ask the equally important question: what do others want and need that I can provide?

It's a question about creating value.

Steve Rutledge is a master of value creation. Past an expected retirement age, he still leads his own marketing consulting business. But his story is less about longevity than it is about blazing new trails. His journey offers good learning about understanding the value you bring to others, whether it's in the world of business or volunteerism.

"Steve, the first thirty years or so of your work life involved a number of job changes."

"You're right about that. After a stint in the Navy, I began my career working for multinational companies including Procter and Gamble, Ralston Purina and Kraft Foods, then started an ad agency focused on the Hispanic market. But these changes weren't as random as they appear. My focus was brand management and marketing, and changes there are inevitable. I did leave P&G after 14 years because I was ready for a fresh challenge, but in the other moves, either the division or the company was sold."

"So, most of the changes came from circumstances I couldn't control. My challenge was how to respond in a way that moved me forward professionally. I read a quote that the best way to predict the future was to create it. Following that idea, my last move 18 years ago involved starting my own company. I was ready to ensure more control over my own future."

"What learning came from those changes that might not have come if your work setting had been more static?"

"I've probably had more experience than many people in asking questions about what I want next, and how to find opportunities. I became very focused on what value I could bring to a given situation and what did I feel differentiated me from competitors."

"I call that 'recalibrating yourself.' For some senior leaders, leaving their companies can lead to their first experience in personal recalibration. It can be an intimidating process because it's unfamiliar.

What advice could you offer them?"

"To answer your question, it might help to track back to my career path from a corporate guy at Kraft, to becoming an agency president, to finally winding up with my own company.

"About the time I decided to part ways with Kraft, I was approached by a group of investors in Puerto Rico that were interested in opening a division in the United States to pursue the U.S. Hispanic Market. They asked me to do a market assessment for them to explore the potential."

"Anyone could have seen that the opportunity was prime. In the early 90's the Hispanic market was exploding, but was new enough that companies didn't know how to reach this population. And I could see a great fit between this client and my experience. The Puerto Rican agency had understanding of the customer; I had been an insider with the kinds of companies in the US this agency wanted as clients."

"So, I joined them to establish the U.S. Hispanic division. My strategy was for this new agency to become a bridge between the two worlds. And it worked spectacularly. In four years we grew the agency from nothing to the 11th largest Hispanic agency in the US and from $0 to $30 million a year in billings at exceptionally healthy profit margins. Companies like Miller Brewing Company, Warner Lambert, Domino's Pizza and AT&T were clients."

"Sounds like one of those perfect matches."

"It was for about five years, until investors in Puerto Rico decided to change directions to a focus on investing in Latin America and the Caribbean. I could see the winds shifting, and knew it was time to redirect myself."

"Did you consider getting another agency position?"

"Sure. And coming off a success like that, I figured I'd be pretty easily employable. But it didn't work that way. I was 57 at the time – not an issue to me, but a powerful issue in the world of re-employment. I learned quickly that recruiters weren't looking for 57-year-olds, and companies tended to think,

'How long will we have this guy? If we hire him, how long will he be around? Is he worth investing in for what may be just a few years?"

"It occurred to me then that bringing value might be more important than the deterrent my age presented."

"If I could demonstrate the value of my experience and perspective from working with many companies either directly or as clients, I felt that people wouldn't care how old I was because I'd be valuable to them. Once I started thinking value, the future looked clearer. For example, I knew consulting firms often sold themselves by touting their Return on Fees. The client might pay $200,000 for a project and realize $5 million in additional revenue or cost savings. A return-on-fees of 25 to 1 is considered quite credible. But in the Hispanic agency, we were able to generate returns of well over 100 to 1. That made for a pretty compelling story."

"However, as I talked with agencies, I began to listen to my own pitch. I had demonstrated outstanding results. Why wasn't I doing this in the context of my own company? From that question, Chicago Associates Management Consultants was born."

"So here you were at 57 years of age with a brand new company in the works. How did you think about its focus?"

"I already knew there were customers who would pay for my services and experience. So I had the freedom to stop and ask myself how I wanted to position my firm."

"By virtue of my work at Kraft and with the Hispanic agency, I was known as an advertising specialist, but frankly, I did not want to be that specialized. I wanted more intellectual satisfaction, to be able to tackle diverse challenges and solve different kinds of problems. That meant creating a company with a more general offering, general management consulting with consumer products and services companies in the areas of strategy, marketing and sales. That was it, in one sentence.

And that's been pretty much it for the last 18 years."

"Any regrets about that choice?"

"None. However, marketing guy that I am, I never stopped paying attention to the environment."

"About four years ago, I found myself asking again, 'How can I better distinguish myself and bring unique value?' And I found an answer by going back to the work I'd done in the Hispanic market. I did some research on the current landscape of the potential of that market, then began purposefully touting my experience and successes in this area with companies. And as a result, four of the last five projects I've done have had to do with the Hispanic market."

"And I needed to recalibrate my value proposition again and even a little differently a couple of years ago when business slowed down considerably. The 2008 financial crisis caused a lot of companies to cut back on discretionary spending–i.e., consulting -, and larger consulting firms like McKinsey began to go after some of the same mid-size firms that had been my sweet spot."

"But it's all about bringing value, right? So last summer I started looking at smaller companies that had the same problems the larger ones did but lacked the resources to address the problems. These smaller companies might be more likely to bring in outside help. Turns out I was on to something, and options for diversification opened up in working with family-owned businesses, and in smaller entities in areas outside traditional consumer packaged goods."

"It doesn't sound like you are slowing down at all."

"Not in the least – I like solving new business challenges. But I think the fact that I'm still at this, and still enjoying it comes from a fairly good knowledge of myself. My wife pointed out recently that from her view, I am always up for helping new clients solve their business problems and bringing my experience to bear on their issues. It seems to keep me intellectually charged."

"I also believe she's hit on what I think is the big question about whether or not others ought to do what I'm doing. They'd do well to ask themselves, 'Am I up for this? And for how long?"

"It's like this. When you go into the market to sell your services and the client may well be in his or her 30s or 40s and assumes anyone in his late 50's can't have something of value to offer and doesn't return your calls...well, it takes pretty thick skin to put up with that lack of common courtesy. You have to be able to relate to younger people in terms of talking about the future and not just the past and to be able to articulate in their language the value you bring. It helps to have both the physical and emotional energy to keep at it."

"And you've got to keep yourself from falling prey to feelings of failure. When I start ruminating about why I did not win an assignment, I sometimes just have to step back and analyze what I could have done differently. The approach was good enough; the proposed program was good enough. For reasons I couldn't control, it just wasn't the time for the company to move. You absolutely can't doubt yourself and lose your self-confidence."

"Instead of focusing on success or failure I look instead at what I learned from experiences. This kind of mental discipline and commitment to experiment is probably a reason why I'm still in the game."

"How long will you still enjoy this?"

"As long as I can see that my work is making a difference, I'll stay at it. Recently, I worked with a large, category leader in food products to expand their penetration of the U.S. Hispanic market. The research suggested that with the right focus they could grow that market in the US to a size comparable to their entire international division. They listened, and we were able to double their sales to over $500 million in just three years. That's the kind of impact that keeps me at this work."

"Maybe in time I'll transition to directing my marketing experience into supporting a cause I believe in. Currently, I'm working with an urban prep school that serves low-income families, helping line up funding for scholarships and mentoring individual students. This is the type of activity that is very satisfying to me and could cause me to shift away from a single-minded focus on working with for profit organizations. However, I do find that the slower pace of that work, and the more limited capacity to make things happen isn't very comfortable for me. So, that's an indicator this might not be the time to make a shift away from a business."

"You're so open to options. How do you do it?"

"I keep this quote from British writer C.S. Lewis on my desk as a great reminder: 'You are never too old to set another goal or to dream a new dream.'

Takeaways to Consider

- Think hard about how and where you can add value.
- A wide perspective including both limitations and opportunities can help you choose a path where you will bring the greatest value.
- Be aware of how others see your experience and insights.
- Ongoing re-evaluation as circumstances change allows for course adjustment and longevity.
- Think about how important it is to you to feel good about what you do—is your work truly helping make an organization better? Are you helping develop the organization by helping people grow?

Questions to Ask Yourself

- How do I create value for others?
- What are some skills or knowledge I might need to add or amplify for the non-profit world?
- What are the ways I can engage a new team before imparting sweeping change?

LIFE 2.0

THE PARTNER

Connie Swartz and Barry Morris
Barbara Allan and Bob Allan

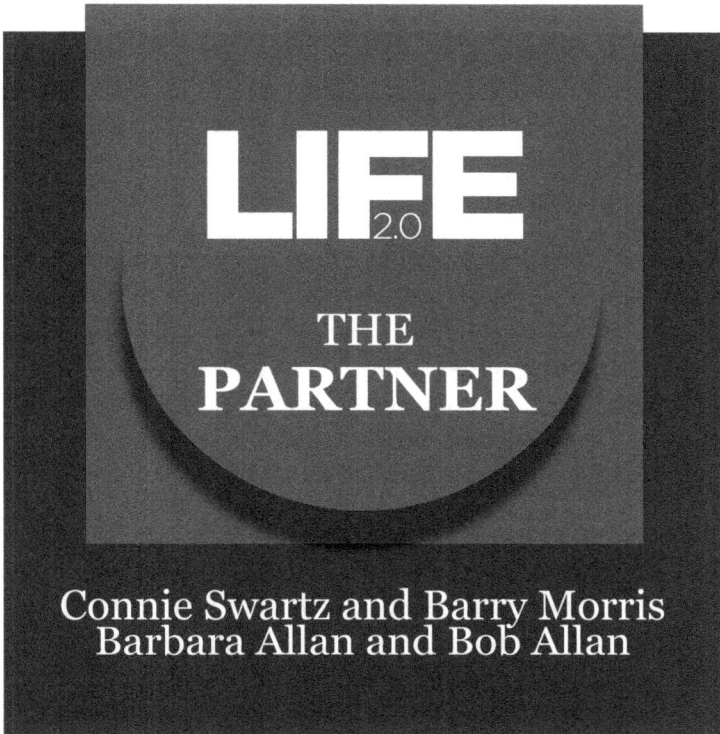

Quote attributed to a grumpy wife who has tired of her husband always being underfoot: “I married you for better or worse, but not for lunch.”

We’ve heard this one-liner often enough it is no longer funny.

But I think the joke has staying power because most of us have a life partner whose schedule and preferences and expectations matter deeply to us. This person with whom we share life factors heavily into the options we consider as we look ahead.

In my interviews, the issue of retirement and cohabitation renegotiations surfaced frequently, even though I hadn’t asked. I learned collaborative life adjustments fell generally into two categories.

Some described the challenges of logistical integration: getting two ways of doing things in sync. One wife said, "Our work required considerable physical separation; of necessity, he went his way; I went mine. Our proximity was emotional, not physical. So, many decisions that involved sharing space and schedules just weren't a daily part of our lives. Now they are."

But a more complex adjustment may lie in companionship expectations. One interviewee told me, "She expected that when I retired, we'd spend all our time together–shopping, doing things with the grandkids, all that. But I was pretty comfortable with the amount of togetherness we had before. And the time we were spending with our grandkids worked well for me, too. We've got big differences to resolve."

Another retiree laughed when he heard this. "My problem is just the opposite," he confessed. "I'm the one who wants to go and do and travel and meet new people. Her idea of a great life at this point is centered on quiet and lack of commitments. Question is, how much of this new life we're organizing is going to be spent together and how much in the company of others?"

However, for some, this question of partnership is more pressing, and more fraught with both opportunities and challenges than for others.

I think of Barbara Allan, and her husband Bob, who function as both life and work partners. Living and working in a collaborative experience creates for them, and others like them, some unique ways of thinking about problem solving as they contemplate changes.

Another set of life partners is Barry Morris and Connie Swartz. The work partnership between these two has been parallel rather than integrated, like Barbara and Bob. The fact that they are both starting new businesses will make some adjustments easier in Life 2.0, but others more complex.

Meet Barbara Allan and husband Bob

Barbara owns a market research business; her husband Bob worked as an electrical engineer for a utility company for 24 years and now is part of Barbara's business.

A major difference between them is this: Barbara's hobby is work; Bob has a variety of hobbies, some of which he'd like to share with Barbara. He loves travel and enjoying their vacation cabin in the mountains of North Carolina. But her commitments as CEO limit her availability."

"Tell me more about some of the challenges of working and living in partnership."

"Not surprisingly, one challenge has to do with differing priorities. Even when we're in North Carolina, I work. I may be out for a morning jog, but I can't stop to chat with neighbors because I might be squeezing in exercise between conference calls. Bob is not as intensely work-driven and struggles with my lack of availability to pursue more shared interests outside of work."

"But a couple we met in North Carolina serve as a caution to me when partners come up against differences like this. They are from Wisconsin. The husband wanted to retire and move somewhere with a more temperate climate. The wife had a fantastic job she loved and deeply missed life where they came from. Now she's pushing to move back. So watching them we saw how important it is to plan changes very carefully when the lives of the two of you are as intertwined as ours are."

"Bob is extraordinarily bright and was very successful in the energy industry. So he brings so much to my company because he understands how to create stability and profitability in the business. And he's a master of measurement to drive accountability. But in his current life view, work is part of the equation, but not all of it. For me, there's more of a single focus on work that he doesn't share."

So, what are you learning about making changes?"

"I think his push to make life a more exploratory experience is a good balance for me. So I'm trying yoga and looking for more options in serving on boards that interest me. And we're becoming quicker to take vacations, like the Baltic Cruise we just completed. Those are changes."

"What do you expect you shouldn't change?"

"We do work and live together, but interestingly, we still maintain some separation – more than some couples I know. I drive my own car to work, and some days I don't interact with him at work because what we're each doing doesn't overlap. We have enough space in our lives that at the end of the day, I often ask, 'So how was your day?' We haven't been together enough – or at all sometimes – so that I'd automatically know. Blending togetherness and separation seems to keep the partnership working well."

Meet Barry Morris and Connie Swartz

Barry Morris and Connie Swartz worked in different businesses. So I asked them to each talk individually about their views on changing their work lives. Then they came together for a dialogue about their shared adjustment during this time of change.

A Conversation with Barry Morris

Barry Morris is a serial entrepreneur. He's been in broadcasting, video production, and now free-lance writing and teaching. However, in all these experiences, it wasn't a matter of simply applying for an existing job; Barry took what he saw and what he wanted in the world of work, and combined these two to make something more.

"The story of your work life could be titled 'A History of Hustle.'"

"I guess it could, and I started early. An interest in ventriloquism led me to child-performer gigs. Along the way I was coached by Jimmy Nelson and was mentored by Edgar Bergen. I worked my way through college as an entertainer."

"Then, during graduate school in Oklahoma, a journalism-major friend who also worked as a radio disc jockey suggested I apply for a job reading news. Two-and-a-half years later, I had leveraged that small start into documentaries, feature pieces, and hosting a late-night music show. We tagged it as 'music to study by' but everyone knew we were providing a soundtrack for, ahem..., many other purposes."

"All this happened during the Vietnam Era, and like so many others, I got my draft notice, then wound up in Turkey in communications. But when word got to my commander that I'd worked in radio, I was soon assigned the management of the military post's broadcasting system and publication of a newspaper."

"After the military, I was determined to get back into broadcasting, but this time to pursue television. With no experience, I picked locations that looked interesting–Denver, Tulsa, Kansas City – and hit the streets pitching myself. A news director at Channel Four in Kansas City decided to offer me a low-level editor position, adding, 'If this works out, we might put you in line for a reporter job...' That beginning led to eighteen years as a mainstay in news reporting for the Kansas City area."

"A change in station management generated the need for a career shift, so I packed up my television experience and moved to writing and producing video-based programming for medical conventions. The work fit well for some twenty years."

"So you must be nearing retirement. Are you still doing that work?"

"Ah, no. That stint is over. Market shifts changed the appetite for this product, so now I'm in the process of not retiring. I'd be bored out of my skull if I didn't work!"

"What's ahead, since you are officially 'not retiring'?"

"This time I'm putting together a collection of work and income streams. 'Words by Barry' is a freelance writing service where I ghostwrite blogs. And I've joined the online faculty of the University of Phoenix, teaching their capstone communications course. Both work streams allow for income, flexibility and creativity, the three things that matter most right now."

A Conversation with Connie Swartz:

Connie Swartz is in the process of selling the training development company she spent the last 30-plus years growing. Starting with a background in instructional design, she leveraged her experience to create a successful business with longevity that is outlasting her leadership.

"How do you feel about letting go of a business you created and grew yourself?"

"Great! I've never understood why people have difficulty delegating. I love to have somebody else do the work. They often do it better than I do."

"Question is, what now?"

"I've taken three months off."

"Just three months? And in those three months you are...?"

"I'm hemming my niece's wedding dress, moving us from our current home to the one-story-house set-up all our friends are choosing, and working on a business plan. Oh, and keeping up with my network of business connections."

"Doesn't sound like you are planning to spend the next twenty years on a beach somewhere sipping pina coladas."

"The twenty years on a beach somewhere doesn't sound bad, but I do obviously have business ideas in mind."

"My idea is focused on developing a subscription home care

service. Not home health care but actually care for your home itself. I'm envisioning people signing on for a monthly or quarterly service where repair people visit regularly to fix what needs attention."

"It will be a fit for those who either can't or just don't want to do their own repairs. And for the repair people, it will allow them to do the work they're trained to without having to manage the marketing and accounting end of work like this."

Obviously these two see 'retirement' as just a way to work differently. They now have new opportunities to apply lessons learned about living and working in a collaborative life.

Barry and Connie talk together about retirement and their partnership:

"Hearing your future plans could suggest two people who maintain separate lives; he does his business, she does hers, with occasional moments of intersection to sync up holiday plans or decide on your dinner destination. Do you basically just live life on two parallel tracks?"

"You wouldn't suggest that if you saw our home office," Barry explained.

"Our desks are no more than ten feet apart. We know some people wouldn't be able to deal with that one."

"Why does this work for you?"

"We're both entrepreneurs, so we've been extremely good support for each other. We know when to be cheerleaders and when to step back and keep our mouths shut. Connie is my sounding board–she's blunt and almost all the time right in her recommendations. Me? I'm much more diplomatic. Maybe my point of view matches hers, but I work to express it more carefully. Both approaches are useful; it's just a matter of what fits the situation."

"It also works because we agree on some big things that are

important to us. For instance, both of us love travel and look forward to having it as an increased focus in the years ahead. Plus, we love what we call 'more comfortable' travel–business class seats when we fly over water, nicer hotels, amenities that cost more, so continued income helps allow for these personal perks."

"But it doesn't mean we are alike on everything," Connie said. "I want a low-maintenance business that doesn't require I be hands-on every day. But Barry is more interested in being able to choose who he will work with. And for him it's especially important to be able to keep learning in ways that teaching young people through the University of Phoenix is providing."

"Somewhere along the line, you two have figured out how to deal with differences. Was this always easy for you? What were the bumps along the way as you got to the smooth flow you have now?"

"If you had visited us about a week after I moved my office into our home, you'd have questioned how well we were dealing," Connie laughed. "Barry had his desk tucked into a dormer in the corner of the room, but my stuff filled up the rest of the space – literally. Think a big copier, a fax, a printer, a workstation, a worktable and a whole lot of boxes. For a while he had to navigate a little path through all this stuff to just get to his desk. It took a while to go through it all, organize it, and move most to the basement."

"But we survived. Now we are on to the everyday business of negotiating working together in a relatively small space. For example, we soon discovered we couldn't be on the phone at the same time. The solution to that one was headsets, so whoever was taking a call could move to another part of the house."

"And an upside of sharing a work space is each of us knowing what the other is working on. Plus, unless one of us is going out, we have lunch together most days. But since we've both been entrepreneurs, we do understand that when one of us has a deadline and disappears on a Saturday to the office, it's not a problem."

"What advice might you have for couples who are moving into the changes this point in life can bring?"

"I think part of why this works well is because we decided what kind of life we wanted before we decided what work we would commit to," Connie explained. "That approach makes the shared decisions much easier."

Takeaways to Consider

- Sharing ideas and mutual goals help shape a balanced future.
- Independent activities that reflect your interests keep both partners energized.
- Finding common ground and respecting differences will smooth the transition path and allow flexibility to meet challenges and exploit opportunities.

Questions to Ask Yourself

- Am I talking about the future with my business and/or life partner?
- Do I know the expectations others (business partners, life partner, clients, employees) have of me?
- Do I understand my partner's goals, priorities, and operating style?
- Have we set milestones for making changes along the path?
- What is my next big idea and what is my plan for it in the context of my partnership?

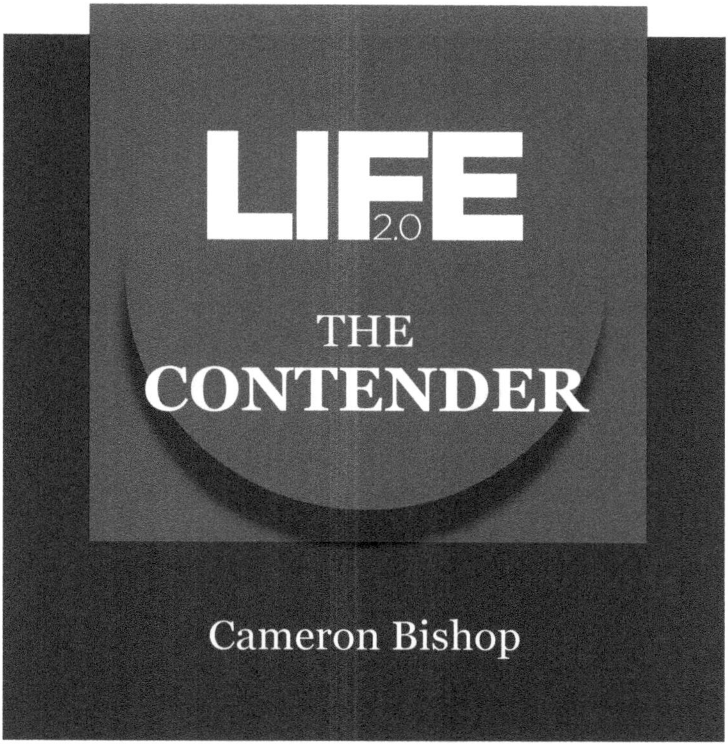

Baseball players, boxers, and politicians: all contenders in that they compete or campaign to win something. And contender has a slightly different connotation than competitor. It implies a more vigorous, even scrappier sense of going at unexpected challenges.

It's this definition that causes me to label Cam Bishop a contender. Cam led several large media companies, enough so that one might expect moving to a life outside this corporate world would come easily. But Cam's change to a role in consulting involved a process of observation, searching, study, analysis, networking, learning, and experimenting before he created a life setting that works the way he wanted it to.

History is particularly instructive and encouraging, for all who don't seem to simply "fall into" the next opportunity. Sometimes that wonderful opportunity has to be created by applying business smarts and tenacity. On both counts, Cam Bishop shows the way.

"Cam, you ran media-oriented companies headquartered in the Kansas City area for some thirty years. What led you to consider a change?"

"For a lot of those years, I lived the life of a 'corporate refugee.' The companies I led usually had a client base elsewhere, so I spent most of my work life on the road. For example, when running a four hundred million dollar company here, less than one percent of my revenues came from businesses in this market. I once counted up that I've made more than 700 trips to New York. Literally."

"So travel, both in the US and internationally, was a way of life. Besides being on the road and working monster hours, there was only time left for family, and no time for volunteering or networking. No time for much of anything else, really."

"Sounds both rich and exhausting."

"You're right on both counts, but exhausting won out. I'd just finished a five-year engagement working on private equity-backed business and told myself, 'That's enough. I don't want to do this pressure-cooker pace again. I have to do something else.'"

"It sounds like removing yourself from business was never an option in your thinking. So, as you looked toward a change of work setting, what surprises confronted you?"

"First, I didn't realize that being a sixty-year-old white male who'd held the title of CEO for nearly thirty years doesn't increase your available options; it shrinks them."

"I hadn't looked for a job since I left college so not only were my networking skills rusty, I started with a poorly-developed network to draw from. Plus, the media industry in which I'd worked is on the decline, thanks to changes in the economy and the predominance of internet-driven communications. In the last 6 to 7 years, over 65,000 jobs have gone away. And the kinds of senior-level jobs for which I was most qualified are now going to people who come from a purely digital background. That wasn't me."

"Did you consider leading in a different industry?"

"Of course. It seemed to me that my leadership and strategic experience would be useful many places. But as I searched, I soon discovered that hiring managers rarely understand the value of skills like creating corporate culture, communicating a vision, identifying, recruiting and retaining top talent–all some of the most difficult skills to develop in a top executive. So emphasis is instead placed on highly industry-specific skill sets and programmed into algorithm-driven HR systems. Since people like me can't match all the keywords, we don't make it through even initial screenings in the search process.

"I began to think you could be a serial killer who could demonstrate that experience in 27 detailed categories and become a candidate."

"Plus, the competition for available positions was beyond fierce. On executive search sites it wasn't unusual to see 200-300 applicants for a position."

"So you stepped back and took a look at your strategy."

"I did. And I have to say the choice to revaluate was a bit of a painful process. I spent an entire career building an experience base and a legacy, and creating a life plan and vision, and now found myself looking down a road I didn't envision...

"Well, I saw I could either let it get me down or make lemonade from lemons. Though the answer seems evident, it didn't come without a process of soul-searching."

"This juncture was as much an emotional exercise as it was cognitive."

"Right."

"But you chose lemonade."

"I did choose lemonade. And I knew that choice meant I'd have to take a deeper look at my options. I thought more carefully about the skills and experience that had led to the titles and roles I'd had. From that evaluation, management consulting emerged as useful application for what I did well."

"Once that decision to consult seemed clear, what were your next challenges?"

"A friend advised, 'Your work is far more likely to come from someone you know than someone you don't.' So I decided I'd better get to know more people."

"It wasn't actually that I didn't know people. I was pretty well recognized in my industry because the company I led had been high-performing. So I'd served on the executive committee of national boards, and had spoken probably 30 or 40 times as an expert or keynote. I'd been written up and quoted in numerous books on industry subjects."

"But my brand wasn't separate from the company's brand. In the world of management consulting, I had no brand other than myself. And I knew from those years running a media company, I was going to have to market myself as a brand."

"Another challenge became clear to me. To sell a brand, you have to define your customer set. But in management consulting, identifying your customers is a little like finding a needle in a haystack. I saw I was going to have to move from a demand-driven marketing perspective to a referral-driven strategy. I was going to be dependent on referrals from other industry professionals to identify potential costumers and to get started establishing relationships with them."

"Sounds to me like it's all about who you know."

"It wasn't that I couldn't sit down and interact. I like people. But when the goal is business referrals, I realized I'm just one microscopic part of others' lives, so it was critical I write that fine-tuned thirty-second elevator pitch to create some degree of memory about me and what I do. Otherwise others are not equipped to function as a surrogate sales person when a potential need comes to their attention."

"So, even though I'd run companies with 2000 employees and dealt with Fortune 10 companies and negotiated multi-million dollar deals and trade venture deals in foreign countries, this old dog needed to learn some new tricks."

"How did you learn those 'new tricks'?"

"I paid for and devoted study time to courses in networking and how to leverage LinkedIn as a process for lead development. Then I called on my skills and experience in advertising, marketing and social media to create a broader profile and footprint and began managing contacts."

"I was out to create a structure where I could become for other people what I call the 'I know a guy.' Everybody likes to help others, I reasoned, so if they hear of a need and can make a reliable recommendation, everybody wins."

"Now, in the management consulting world, people I meet may not run across a scenario where they get to say, 'I know a guy...' and make a referral for a year or more. So my next challenge was this: how could I maintain some kind of ongoing awareness in people's heads so they didn't quickly forget me? How can I become more generally known as a leader in the consulting specializations I'm developing?

"For me, the answer that made sense was content channels–creating content and publishing that into multiple channels. I created a blog and posted it through a WordPress account, LinkedIn, Twitter, and now through the corporate LinkedIn site representing The Capitus Group, which I joined. I'm also working on a presentation to use on a speaking tour to Chambers of Commerce or Rotary Club meetings, or any other related industry business meetings."

"So during this process, you decided to join a consulting firm, rather than go it alone. What made this group a fit for you?

"The consulting group I joined was fairly new when I discovered it and still recruiting its senior consultants. It was developed to bring together very senior executives with different types of expertise that could be pooled when client needs suggested it. So the fit for my experience was there. And because the company was young when I became a part, I could help shape its direction."

"The firm was created to help business owners who are trying to figure out whether to sell their company or transition it to the next generation. Both have challenges. But I've spent much of my professional life buying and selling companies and integrating those companies, so I knew the work."

"Choosing this company was a starting point, not an ending point. Now my challenge became helping the company become a leader in our area of specialization, beginning with the contacts and networks we have."

"But since the company is young, getting known and consequently developing a rich base of clients doesn't happen immediately."

"That's a given. In an area like ours -management consulting building a company like this isn't going to be an overnight venture."

"And I could see early on that doing well at service delivery wasn't going to be an overnight venture for me personally, either. Besides getting clients, it took time to learn how to do a new business. In the build-up stage (I joined in September and completed my first project in April), I did good work and gave good value. But because I was learning, the project actually took about twice as many hours as I billed for. But I wanted to be sure the work was right, so starting with a loss leader was okay with me. Of course, that approach didn't produce the same level of income for the time invested as it does now that I'm more experienced."

"What's different as you look at where you are now compared with what you used to do?"

"Well, for one thing, income predictability is different as a consultant than it was as an employee. Management consulting is an economically unreliable business by its very nature. It's feast or famine. You could be working eighty hours one week and have no work the next. Every management consultant I spoke with as I considered doing this kind of work told me to set up an alternative source of income that's reliable. So, on the side, I'm creating a start-up in the fitness industry to create a second income stream."

"And, as far as the work, it's different to be an advice-giver rather than the one responsible for execution. Consultants give advice; company leaders either act on the advice themselves or get others to. I miss executing. I like the outcome of execution enough that if I woke up one morning and someone offered me an incredible job running a company again, I would probably seriously consider it."

"But the tradeoff is that now I control my time. Now I have autonomy and flexibility I never had. My last job was so demanding I probably took off Christmas Day or Thanksgiving, but otherwise I took no vacations for a year and a half. Life is too short to do that anymore! And now I pick up my 3-1/2 year old granddaughter from day care. It's wonderful. My wife and I even went with friends to a Royals baseball game during the day yesterday."

"But I have to monitor this flexibility thing more than I did when I was in corporate. For instance, my home gym is right next to my office. I've always been a morning workout person, so my plan was to continue the routine I'd had for years: get the workout done first thing, and then start my workday. But with the office right next to my exercise stuff, it's too easy to say, 'I should send out that email.' Before I know it, it's 10 a.m.; I'm still emailing, and the workout didn't get finished."

"The major positive in your current work is flexibility; a negative is being part of the problem-solving, but not being able to manage execution of the solution to a satisfactory end. Are there other challenges?"

"I think the more subtle challenges center on responding to recurring crises of confidence. I wonder from time to time, 'Am I doing the right thing? Is this the best approach? What might I be missing?' And it has taken courage to confront my own fear of failure. When I made the decision to start a business and change my career track, the levels of unknown grew exponentially. It's not possible to succeed without making a commitment to the new direction, but that new commitment also comes with pressure. Some of the work isn't fun, of course, and some of the unknowns are economic, which can be scary."

"But I remind myself that I'm calling the shots; every day I create plans and problem solve."

"I have to remember that starting a business is like creating a painting, which is one of my hobbies."

"When I start a painting it's actually kind of painful because I'm not quite sure where I am going. I have a vision, but I'm not sure how to get there. But I have to start laying down paint and then change it. Or sometimes it starts going in the direction I thought, but then the direction seems to shift and I have to adapt, adding different colors than I imagined. You start to put the paint on the canvas and at first it doesn't look like anything. But eventually it's going to be a great picture.

"Like building the new business, it's a creative process and I love the result, but getting there can be uncomfortable. So, just acknowledging discomfort is part of the process helps me remind myself to enjoy it."

Takeaways to Consider

- The courage of honesty about your background and challenges is a strong asset.
- It is OK to be uncomfortable – enjoy the process rather than be diminished by what you need to learn.
- Pursue your networking relentlessly, with strategy, and create teams that best fit the problem you are solving.

Questions to Ask Yourself

- How can I make lemonade from lemons?
- How might I learn new tricks?Do I go it alone or find a team?
- How might I find my best creative and strategic collaborators?
- What role is best for me–investigator, planner, or implementer?

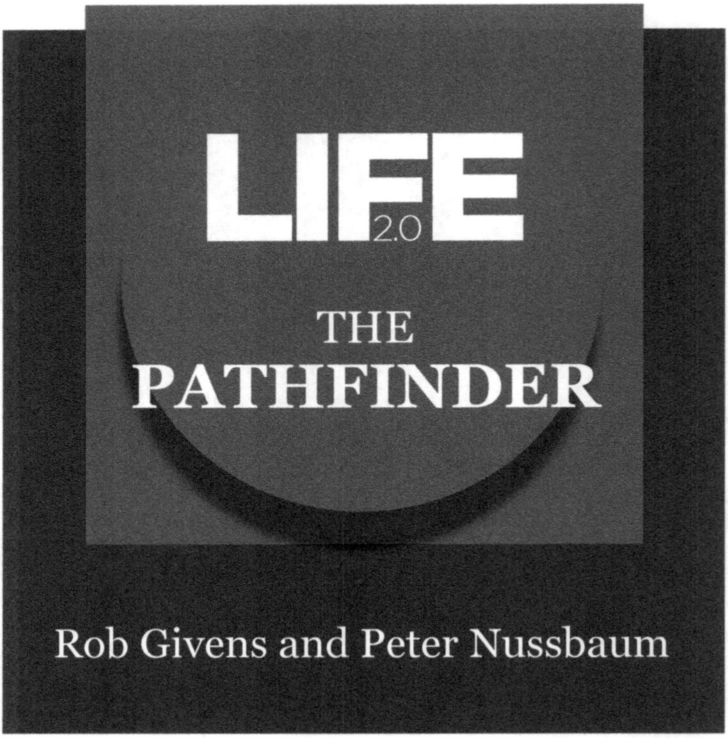

One of the most common comments I heard from interviewees was this: "I'm going to have to find a way to work after I retire from this job. My hobby is work."

Many of my subjects kept working because they simply loved it. There was no need to abandon work to find something they enjoyed doing. Perhaps they wanted a less demanding schedule or more time off, but the current format of their lives was not a curse. Instead, a curse for them would lie in facing day after day of no one needing them, no one recognizing them, no one seeking them out.

However, two of my interviewees looked at retirement options through a very different lens. Both left high-demand jobs they enjoyed without looking back, and chose instead new time investments wrapped around volunteering, travel and developing long-neglected parts of themselves.

Their stories explain how they came to this decision and facilitated the transition from high-intensity, high profile professionals to create new and satisfying lives for themselves.

A Conversation with Rob Givens

"You started fairly early – earlier than most – in thinking about your retirement."

"I did–ten years before it happened, actually. When I became CEO of the credit union at 56, I purposefully decided then that I'd have a ten-year run. In my own mind I put a stake in the ground. And within a year when we were negotiating my retirement package, I tied my retirement to that date as well. The commitment was clear that I'd get on my horse and ride off into the sunset."

"This choice is more unusual than it first appears. Many of those I've spoken to were determined to keep their options open. Why did it seem important to you to establish a date?"

"My first 'employment' situation was twelve years with the Air Force. There I first saw the people we called 'ROAD Warriors' –which to us meant 'Retired On Active Duty.' In other words, they still had jobs; they drew a salary. But they didn't work to full capacity because it wasn't insisted upon, and they could see the end in sight. I never wanted to be one of those people."

"Another factor was at play. After the military, I led in organizations where I saw leaders push hard for their agenda to the last day of their tenure. Their successors were left to manage an organization shaped by the predilections and preferences and style of their predecessor. That seemed neither fair to the successor nor good for the organization, to my mind. So I started a year before my intended leave date to work with the Board on choosing a successor."

"During that last year, did you spend time thinking about the days following your retirement?"

"Not specifically. But I remember thinking, 'I finished college 46 years ago – I've been working a long time. Now it's time to go and play. I have resources and time I didn't have previously, and things I would like to do...it's time to go after them!"

"Were you thinking specifics?"

"Well, I knew it wouldn't be golf five days a week. Fine game, but I've always been driven to keep growing as a person, and I couldn't see golf offering challenges that would let me do that. Instead, I pictured travel and reading as starting places. Beyond that, I looked forward to exploring options and seeing how it all unfolded."

"I hear from others you've pursued your travel interest aggressively. It sounds like in the last four years, you've seen a lot of the world."

"We, my wife and I, have seen our share. But I want to put that aggressive travel decision in context. Our motivation for seeing the world is different from some. We've met people who are making checkmarks behind every UNESCO site and National Park. The power of visiting these places seems to lie in being able to say, 'I've seen that one.' Sort of a 'been there, done that,' mentality."

"That's not what drives us. I have a rampant curiosity. My family has owned a summer cottage in Michigan since 1936. I spent summers there as a child, and took our kids there as they were growing up. But when the kids were about 15 or 16, something shifted for me. I told my mom, 'I love this place; it has a deep emotional attachment for us. But the world has so much to offer we haven't seen.' And the next year my wife and I went to Europe for the first time. The determination to explore hasn't stopped since."

"And for me it's more than just a drive to have adventures, like climbing the Eiffel Tower or seeing the Pyramids. Reading Stephen Hawking on string theory and quantum mechanics gave me a new view of travel from the view of the continuity of life. Now, somewhere on each trip I find myself thinking,

'These people who seem so different from me have been living here, are living here and will continue to live here well after my visit. And they are doing the same day-to-day slog here that I do in my world.' Seeing our sameness gives me perspective and empathy that makes learning about them immediate and gratifying. It's not an academic exercise for me; it's a growth exercise."

"For us, we shouldn't travel unless we are willing to let the travel change us."

"So do you visit places more than once?"

"Not usually, because there's so much more we want to learn about. But there's a caveat to that. We've heard in some of the places that we visited that the location is very different at a different time of year, or something important has changed in the location. For instance, we went on safari in Africa in January, during the rainy season. People said it was a different world than in September in the middle of dry season, when the animals flock to the watering holes. So a different season there would result in some new learning. That's the intention."

"You are very clear on travel-as-learning."

"We are. That's one reason we chose a tour company that offers very small groups – ten or twelve, usually, and "day-in-the-life" experiences in local people's homes rather than just seeing the tourist-focused sights. And the travel company's foundation contributes to school and other improvements in the areas where they host tours. So we become aware of needs and ways to help while we are enjoying amazing exposure to new cultures. It's a best-of-both-worlds thing, from my view."

"Along with all this travel, you are pretty active as a volunteer. How did that decision come about?"

"You can't travel all the time! Like everyone, we need roots and stability. So the question became, while we are home, how will we spend our time? Will it be just watching TV and reading, or is there some place we can contribute? So we began looking for opportunities that seemed to meet those needs.

"During the years leading the credit union it turned out I found more than a job; I found a passion. The credit union was originally organized to serve federal employees and their families. And it happened that many of these came from lower socioeconomic settings, so we found that 30-40% of our members were from the lower income spectrum. One of my early assignments was opening a branch office in midtown; our credit union was coming in while other banks were fleeing this blighted area. As it turned out, we became the only banking resource for this underserved population."

"Though there were days when I wondered what I had gotten into, I found that offering resources to these folks really captured me. I wound up being president of some boards that served that area, so my learning and exposure grew deeper. During my ten years with that credit union, I discovered that my heart was in helping these people. That passion for helping this community led right into the volunteer things I've chosen to do now."

"What kinds of boards did you subsequently choose after retirement?"

"It won't surprise you to learn I'm working with a coalition of urban and suburban churches and marketplace people who are doing economic and community development in depleted neighborhoods. And I'm chair of the board of a community funding group which uses New Market Tax Credits to make development funding to businesses in communities in need."

"It was also a pretty natural segue to join the board of a development group that focuses on housing and community life for the elderly. We focused efforts on communities that are developing walkable neighborhoods, adaptive housing and transportation and caregiving models. We started with an emphasis on seniors, but discovered that Millennials had similar interests, similar needs. So now we've reframed the mission to make it more inclusive."

"And my leadership background and interest in seniors has

recently led me to join AARP lobbying efforts on senior issues. This is also a great complement to volunteer work my wife is doing as an ombudsman for the state, representing the elderly in assisted living and skilled nursing facilities."

"I thought you told me you were retired. Did I miss something?"

"I want to be engaged, not employed. When I say yes to a board, I let them know up front about travel commitments, and that I won't always be available. And I encourage them to not schedule around my availability, though some do anyway."

"But handling multiple commitments isn't all that different from life running a company. And, I'm careful to focus in these jobs on not doing everything, just contributing what I do well – like big picture thinking, for example. I don't know every number on every financial, but I can ask the questions that help to keep the organization moving toward its goals."

"And because as CEO I worked for a board, I keep a clear eye to that Board/Executive Director relationship. It's easy for volunteer boards, that have a lot of passion for a cause, to sometimes try to micromanage the details. If you want to drive an exec crazy quickly, this is a good way! So, I call from my work experience to keep the Board's input and reach at the right level."

"You've mentioned a couple of ways you've repurposed your work experience in the volunteer sector. Are there other ways?"

"There've been some unexpected ways. For example, my work life provided considerable experience in linking potential homeowners to resources they wouldn't have found otherwise. Now, in one community development program we are taking ex-cons and trying to get them loans for homeownership. Really, what institutions are going to lend for that? But, I still know people. And I can go to the local credit union and explain it in their terms. I tell them, 'The regulators won't bother you; the risk isn't that high; and I know your book structure and that you could handle this. Involvement also offers positive PR potential, and if the launch goes bad, we will sign on and carry it until we get someone else into the property so you won't necessarily lose.' Now, that's fun."

"Many tell me they want to serve on Boards. How did you get these opportunities?"

"I found causes I cared about, and let people know I was interested. And I've also adopted a "Say Yes" philosophy – a penchant to experiment. If I'm approached with an opportunity, I tell myself, 'I'll go once and see what they have to offer. I'll see how it feels and whether or not I think it's a fit – then I'll decide.' But I don't say no without giving it a try. And I let them know I can always move on if it's not a fit on my side–or on theirs."

"What would you say to others about your retirement choices?"

"In America, we are blessed to even be able to ask questions about what to do in retirement. In most of the world people don't have this chance. So rather than focusing on retiring in style, we ought to focus on retiring with style. In five or ten years, I want to look back and look at some civic improvements and say, 'Had my fingerprints on that one.' Or 'We wouldn't have come as far as we have in that cause if I hadn't had a role in it somewhere.' It's not the public acknowledgment I need – that's insignificant. It's the sense of making a difference."

A Conversation with Peter Nussbaum

"You were with your law firm for twenty-five years. Had you established a retirement age for the partners?"

"Actually, the partnership agreement provided that after seventy, you could stay in the firm only with the permission of the firm. The provision was in place because another firm had a founder who would not leave, and caused all kinds of problems – they finally had to force him out. We didn't want that. So 'seventy plus only with permission' became our policy."

"So it was the agreement that instigated your thoughts of retirement?"

"Not at all. My wife and I traveled a lot, and after a trip to Antarctica, I came home feeling like I no longer wanted to work full time. I was nearing seventy at the time, but it wasn't the age thing that provoked the idea to change; I could simply tell I was ready."

"So you tendered your resignation and moved on?"

"Not even close. The process took nearly three years from my first conversation to my current situation of going into the office only about one day a week. When I introduced the idea, one of my partners who did not want me to leave said, 'Why not just cut back to 60% or 80% workload? That way you can ease into the idea and still be a partner.' So for a year I committed to three days a week in the office."

"How did it work for you?"

"Poorly. I most often wound up being in the office four or five days; when a big project was in process I worked nearly round the clock. It was just the nature of the work. So I knew we'd have to try something else. The second year, I decided to leave my partnership role and just work hourly. I thought it would give me more latitude in simply taking on what I wanted to and saying no to the rest. I was thinking maybe 15 hours a week doing only projects I wanted to do sounded good."

"And you kept to that plan?"

"Sort of. There was a time during the year that I was working 40-50 hours a week because the project demanded it. But other weeks I didn't work at all, so I averaged about 15 hours a week over the course of the year. I knew I hadn't found the solution yet, but I liked the social contact and occasional professional stimulation with the people in the firm. We needed to try something else. So, now, in Year Three, I'm still a member of the firm – at their request – and go in one day a week."

"What do you do on that day?"

"That depends, but it's very different from before. I go in on Wednesdays because that's when my Pilates class in the city is scheduled. And I schedule lunch with people in the firm, and do other business I need to in San Francisco. And when business issues come up that I know a lot about, I chime in and take on a task. Right now it seems to work."

"What else was important to you as you considered leaving the firm?"

"One of the ways I prepared for leaving the firm, i.e., my succession plan, was never to hog my clients. I always had younger people working with them so that the clients really got to know and trust them. Thus, my leaving the firm was not traumatic for the clients. "

"Pulling back sounds like an iterative process. How are you thinking about shaping this new life?"

"I'm ready to try things, do things there just hasn't been time to do. Like more travel. And reading. Enjoying the newspaper and the New Yorker and history. And before a trip, like the one we took to Rome, I can now study the place we'll visit and go with a different knowledge base. And I've found photography as a growing interest. I've been taking classes, learning new programs. Right now, I'm finding I enjoy travel and photography enough to lose myself in them. I could spend all day wandering through cities and stay up all night working on the photographs."

"You've probably been approached about volunteer opportunities or Board service. Have you thought of repurposing your legal experience to these settings?"

"On the legal question, absolutely not. I contributed well when I practiced law. I'm ready now to try new things. I've been approached about getting involved in politics, but it doesn't interest me. And some foundation work that's been offered doesn't do it either."

"I relished mentoring young lawyers and remember enjoying some of the classes I offered to clients during my professional years. I'm from a family of teachers so I'm naturally thinking about teaching, maybe tutoring kids from disadvantaged settings."

"You eased away from full-time work and now you seem to be in an exploratory mindset."

"I had been told many years ago that a mistake many people make when retiring was having too much planned in advance. It was suggested to give oneself a fair amount of time, maybe a year or even two, to just relax and not be overcommitted in terms of things that had to be done. That's what I've tried to do, and I'm now going through what I call 'small-scale experimentation.' That for me is very important. I've come from 40+ years where every moment was planned and accounted for. That's not what I want now. And the experimentation over time will hopefully help me work out the contours of retirement."

What advice do you have for those who are thinking ahead to retirement?"

"One thing I will never regret: keeping a fairly good sense of balance between work and the rest of life. Even in the years before these, I'd take off a month when we'd travel. We planned the trips a year in advance so when a judge was setting dates for hearings six months out, I could say, 'Sorry. I'm going to be out of the country.' And there was never a problem. Some people opt for deferred living. Not me. One never knows what life has in store for you, so I firmly believe you should do things that are important to you and your spouse.

Takeaways to Consider

- Recognize when you are ready to exit, and consider a plan for either a staged or full departure.
- Whatever you choose, do it with style.
- Think of your roots and the footprint you wish to leave, and explore where you can make a difference.
- Don't be afraid to experiment with new and alternative pursuits.
- Continuous learning keeps you vital and vibrant.

Questions to Ask Yourself

- If I'm intending to exit my role, what is my succession plan?
- How will I transfer my knowledge but leave options for others' preferences?
- What different lenses can I use to broaden my perspective?
- What experiments could I try with new interests or pursuits?

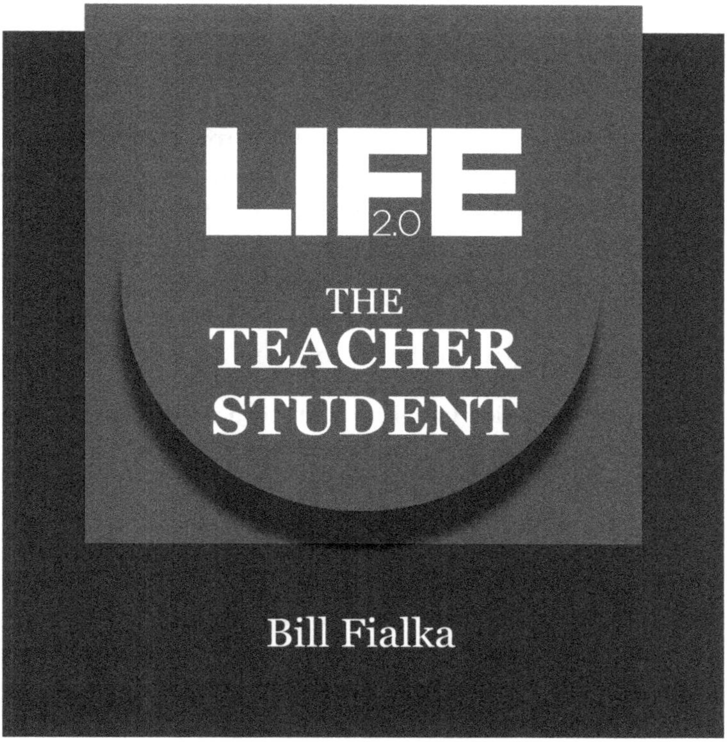

This is the time to do what matters to you. So say many retirement coaches.

And it is, of course.

But what if "what matters to you" isn't all that clear?

Bill Fialka has a story that might lend some ideas to finding that answer. Bill was CEO of a successful ad agency. When he departed, he tried his hand at starting a company, putting out a shingle to see if this option was a fit for him. William Fialka and Associates served customers for a couple of years, then Bill moved to employment with a firm that needed the marketing help he offered.

The rationale and process of a shift like this offers a different way of thinking about finding direction in this retirement process.

"So many retirees I'm talking with are thinking of starting a business. You started one, then left it. How did that come about?"

"It took being on my own to get over the romance of being on my own. And in that experiment, I learned about two parts of myself I'd never seen so clearly. First, I need structure. I learned the hard way that I'd get up in the morning and find forty things to do other than build a business. And by 11:00 a.m. or so I'd be knocking on my wife's office door saying, 'Hey, do you want to go to lunch? Do you want to play some golf?"

"The other big deficit in being on my own was the lack of predictable collaboration. I found I really missed sitting in a room bouncing ideas off other people–seeing what we could create together, and then executing on those ideas as part of a team."

"It had seemed so reasonable to me, that after thirty years of business experience, I would thrive as a sole proprietor. And structure? The capacities to be accountable and to create a collaborative environment and lead a team were a big part of my success in the past. I've been the CEO of a marketing firm, for Pete's sake! Surely I could make a solo business work."

"I spent some time in denial, but when I finally faced facts the truth seemed very simple: I do better as part of a team. This business of going it alone isn't where I succeed most easily."

"So what did you do?"

"Ah, I joined a small service company that had been around thirty years and had never done any marketing whatsoever. So, we started them on a Customer Relationship Management System, then got them on Constant Contact to do email marketing. And we're adding some print trade advertising. I expect that by the end of the year we will have the marketing tools they need well in place."

"So, what then? Retirement?"

"Hardly. I've already got my eye on several opportunities–from a very cool tech start-up to a more traditional manufacturing business. In each case, marketing help will really get them where they want to be more quickly. All those years of agency work I did will come to play. I can help them plan and focus on who they want to sell to and how best to structure the business."

"It sounds to me like you don't have much interest in talking about getting ready to retire."

"You heard that right. Retirement scares me. The people I know who have left the business world completely seem to have lost touch with what's going on around them. Plus, I'm not done building something and watching it grow. That excites and fulfills me."

"I have friends walking into this retirement thing, and I've been learning watching some of them that doing nothing isn't all it's cracked up to be. With one buddy who retired, we had to do a little intervention when he was ready for lunch by 11:00 o'clock. My friend was just bored, nothing to do all day. He wanted the people-connections he used to enjoy at his company."

"The confusion was this: my friend has more money than God, so there was no financial need to work. But he needed work. So he bought a business with his brother. He's an avid hunter, so during the non-bird-hunting season, he works with the business, and during the hunting season he heads out to hunt. And his energy for life has come back."

"He's your 'cautionary tale?'"

"I don't know if I'd describe it that way. But I did feel sure I knew what was happening with my friend because of what I'd seen with my dad. When he sold his company, he was home for about sixty days. Now, I don't know what happened to change things, if he decided on his own to change his focus, or if my mom threatened him with death if he didn't get out of the house. However it happened, he started volunteering. Since he was a CPA, he ended up working for a charitable organization and kept at it for another 10-15 years. Those who said he didn't have to work were only looking at his financial position. He did have to work to keep living a happy life."

"So is it always going to be about working for you?"

"Honestly, it isn't just about continuing to hold a job. A good friend of my wife worked in the government sector in a creative position. But as time went on, more constraints limited her ability to create, so she began to hate the job. Toward the end she could tell you to the minute how long she had until retirement."

"But as soon as that day, that minute came she got into golf like a mad woman. She plays at least eighteen holes six days a week or even more than that. She enters every tournament she can and is our club champion. Now, there are better golfers at our club, but there is no one who will outwork her to win. I think it's because she's driven by the need for purpose."

"My non-golfing friends tend to see this as a pretty superficial purpose, but they are missing the point, to my mind. Getting better at golf establishes who she is today. It anchors a sense of worth, which is just a basic human need."

"Do you see my point? We all have to be about something, to be useful for something. When we aren't useful or building anymore, we might as well be dead."

"So, now that money isn't the critical driver anymore, how do you think about where you want to build and contribute? What's that 'Something' you want to be about?"

"I'm guessing most people like me will talk about wanting to help businesses succeed, all of that. One thing that may be different for me is how really deeply drawn I am to young people. Being with them and part of helping them grow and learning from them – it is kind of an addiction, like drugs. Working with them is my 'fix.'"

"How did you come to this discovery?"

"I began to see a pattern in where I was finding energy. First, after my time as a CEO, when people asked what I wanted to do, I heard myself saying, 'I want to continue to work with young people in a creative environment.' The creative environment thing wasn't so surprising – it's the essence of the world of advertising and marketing. But hearing myself call out working with young people as equally important–I took note.

“And I think it’s congruent that I’m drawn to start-ups and small to mid-sized businesses that want to grow; most of these involve young people trying new things. I love hanging out at a local organization called One Million Cups. It’s a gathering place for entrepreneurs who present their concept for feedback. And some of these ideas, well, I think, ‘Oh, Buddy. Don’t quit your day job... But that’s not the point. It’s the fun of all these experimenters who are willing to break out and give it a go.

“I love the energy of young people. Being with them pushes me into learning to apply technology to problems I grew up solving other ways. And I’m very respectful of how they define approval. Their heroes might be typified by someone who is going out to start an organic farm. My generation would hear that and say, ‘What the hell are you going to do to monetize that?’ And the young think, ‘Monetize it? Who cares? She loves doing this!”

“Our generation struggles with that response. But I’m learning from it. It’s a very different way to think about where you make a life investment, but they’re teaching me.”

“What do you want to teach them?”

“I can help them learn to sell themselves–and that’s a skill everyone needs. And to become the best at getting inside their clients’ businesses, to be as passionate about that business as if it was their own. Those are marketing skills, of course, but they are great life skills too that apply to most any kind of work.”

“And, I’m finding there are so many ways to help prepare them for the world. I’m on the board of trustees for my old fraternity. A couple of months ago, we board members designed a 3-hour ‘career counseling’ session for the guys in the frat. It was world-class fun.”

“We started with what we saw as pretty obvious. ‘Clean up your

Facebook page,' we told them. 'Get all those cool pictures of you drinking on the beach off that sucker. Then get on LinkedIn and figure out how to utilize everything you've got with perspective employers in mind. Get personal business cards – you can order them free off the Internet – and when you finish meeting with someone who could hire you, hand them one. You'll separate yourself from the competition, and you need to because there's plenty of competition out there."

"Then we split up the group by their majors and provided a professional from their desired line of work to answer questions. It was a productive free-for all. In the pre-law group, one kid said, 'I'm a political science major, so I can do blah-blah-blah with it.' Sounded impressive to me, but the attorney leading the group broke in. 'Let me stop you right there,' he said. 'I was a poly sci major too. But I didn't know how to write, or know anything about finance or economics. These turned out to be the things I use in my law practice every day. I'd encourage you to rethink your undergrad degree."

"Who gives this kind of advice? The kid was writing notes as fast as he could. The whole experience turned out to be pretty exciting for all of us."

"I see it like this. Our future is in the hands of young people like these. My generation? We're done – we've messed up all we can. It's going to be up to these guys to carry us forward, so if I get to be part of helping them get ready to do that well, I see that as wonderful."

Takeaways to Consider

- Learning from younger people keeps you young.
- Experiment with new modes of work; help others experiment with their enterprises.
- Use your learning to recalibrate your direction.
- There are unlimited ways to mentor others.

Questions to Ask Yourself

- Where do I get my energy?
- How will I keep myself plugged into the people, knowledge, and energy I want?
- What are the ideas I'd like to experiment with?
- What are possible avenues for teaching or mentoring?

LIFE 2.0

THE BUILDER

Delphyne Lomax and Pamela Kelly

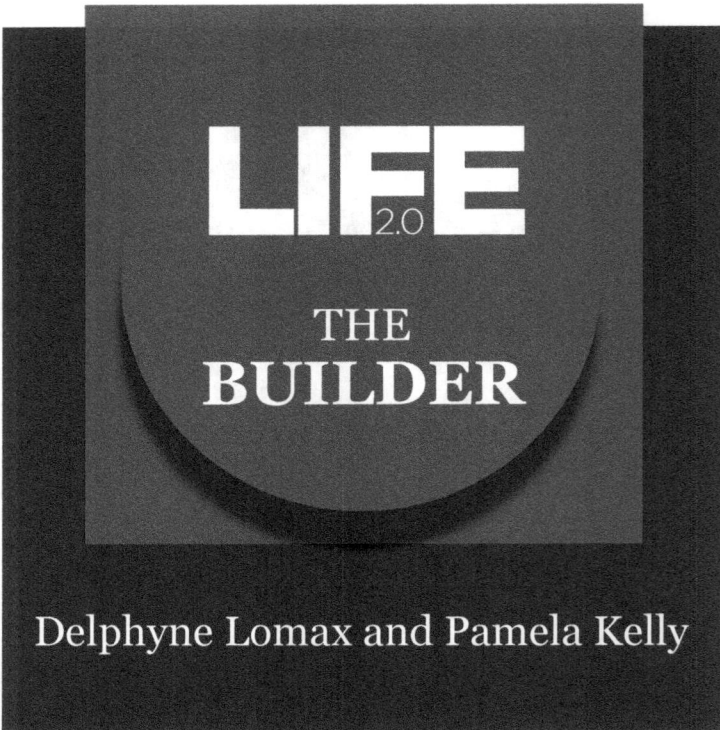

During our twenties and thirties, we speak about 'building a career,' as if it's a phase that has an end as we move into full productivity. In the world of work, we start, we build, we produce and we celebrate. Positioned like this, 'building' sounds like one element of a linear process, one rung on a ladder.

But Delphyne Lomax and Pam Kelley would look at the process of 'building' through a different lens. Though Delphyne grew a successful market research business while Pamela was creating a successful career in the media industry, neither would describe these processes of building as a phase or a life stage.

These leaders are taking the skills and experience they learned in business and refocusing them in new endeavors. And the work they are now choosing opens not just interesting new opportunities for them, but will help to build strength and courage into women and girls.

Delphyne and Pam show us how to build something great for ourselves, and then how to rebuild in ways that make for a better world.

A Conversation with Pam Kelley:

Pam enjoyed the kind of high-flying career many dream about. As an executive in the entertainment industry, she developed a business entity that was doing a billion dollars in gross sales with a workforce of only fifty people.

But in the AOL/Time Warner merger, her division became part of a larger entity, and the new management held little appeal for Pam. She spoke with her financial advisor who said, "Do what you want. You're well-set enough that you don't have to work."

What followed was the creation of an organization to point girls toward careers in politics. A work life focused on business success had transitioned nicely into a focus on meaning.

"How did the move from corporate to starting a not-for-profit come about?"

"Well, the news that income wasn't going to be an issue for me opened the option of following a long time passion for more involvement in politics. So, for the next couple of years, I invested time and energy to help a candidate I believed in get elected."

"Along the way, I joined the board of the Women in Politics Foundation, and a fortunate confluence of events led to my next move. A new source of funding came available to the Foundation. I was Board vice president at the time, and did considerable brainstorming with the president about where we might do the most good with this funding resource.

"Just at this time, my colleague's 6-year-old daughter went to camp."

"As it turned out, the only camps available that would work with everyone's schedules were soccer and princess camps. The girl had no interest in soccer, so her mother reluctantly selected the princess camp. At Parents' Night at the camp's closing, the girls demonstrated what they had learned during the week, 'lessons' that included making a foam crown, and learning to properly curtsy to the king."

"Oh, boy! You can imagine the reaction from both her mother and me! We decided something needed to be done – and that we were the ones to do it."

"Teaching little girls how to curtsy to the king didn't fit your idea of time well-spent?"

"We wondered how it fit anyone's idea of time well-spent!"

How did you come to the idea of a camp?

"During my tenure at Time Warner, I attended a management development seminar for women executives called Breakthrough Leadership. The experience focused on the strengths women bring to leadership, and how to lead authentically with a view to both business and personal life balance. I was deeply impacted, and had told my colleague about it. As we brainstormed alternatives to playing princess, I began to wonder, 'Why aren't we teaching young girls the lessons I learned at that executive seminar? Why couldn't they learn about what constitutes good leadership?"

"After considerable research on what is offered to young girls, we decided to create a camp for 10- to 14- year-olds to provide them with knowledge about leadership and about our government and civic engagement. We selected this age group because the research we explored, suggested that during these years girls' confidence begins to plummet. They are exploring who they are – and will be – in the world, and need to know they are important."

"Encouraging these girls during those vulnerable years to dream big and giving them skills could be a game changer for these girls. And to incite a large vision in them, we decided to call the camp Madam President."

"Our model became a summer camp with two sessions, each at one of two university campuses in town. We'd bring in local girls to participate. Our tag line became: 'We want girls to aspire to be Hillary Clinton or Condoleezza Rice, not Kim Kardashian."

"Starting your own not-for-profit is the dream for so many. Did it work out like you expected?"

"It worked well from a vision perspective. The girls learned to build their own political campaigns, and by the end of the week, speak to their parents, and to others we'd invite to talk about their beliefs and vision."

"We didn't intend it be a civics class–you know, 'Here are the three branches of government.' Instead they meet politicians and women of influence who can serve as models. We wanted to plant the seed of running for office or to becoming the women behind the people who are running for office. Change agents."

"Four years later, the program was well-attended and getting good reviews."

"But from a personal financial perspective, the story was quite different. It was becoming clearer and clearer that our business plan wasn't financially sustainable. Though we charged tuition, it didn't cover expenses, and as creators of a new organization, we felt we needed to give our time to program development rather than fundraising, so to make up the difference, we invested our own money."

"These are the decisions you make when you are passion-driven."

"They are. But what followed these financial realizations involved major adjustments in the structure of Madam President.

"In the organization, my co-founder and I decided to pull back from such aggressive day-to-day involvement. We recreated the business model into one I think may offer even more possibilities for the future. We're turning the work we've done into a curriculum we can then license to other entities, and hiring an executive director who will both manage the organization and fundraise so the program can continue. We are changing the profile of people who will serve on the board, so they can be part of the fund-raising effort, not just advisors. As it turns out, these are all smart steps to ensure sustainability. Getting caught up short financially helped us make these positive moves."

"What have you learned about the keys to making a not-for-profit venture like this work?"

"Part of the answer is logic-based; the other part is heart-based.

"I'd tell others to start with excellent research, the kind you'd do if you were starting any kind of business. You know the questions: Why this business? Who are the competitors? What will it take to make it succeed?"

"But you also have to have passion, something you're ready to devote both time and money to. There'll be many moments when you are tempted to give up, but it's the passion that will keep you going. And it also helps, I think, to have a partner who is as committed as you are. My colleague and I both believed in this so deeply we were able to keep each other going in time of adversity."

A Conversation with Delphyne Lomax:

Delphyne and her business partner have run a successful market research firm for more than twenty years.

Life and work seemed to be churning along at a rapid but comfortable clip.

That was until the day that her husband told her he no longer wanted to be married to her. Apparently he'd always felt lost in her shadow and was looking for a different life and life partnership."

Then, about three years later came the breast cancer diagnosis. Surgery followed, and thirty rounds of radiation plus three months of chemotherapy. Experiences she never imagined would be part of her life.

Now in her mid-fifties, a path that had seemed predictable for the next ten to perhaps twenty years needed adjustments. The builder needed to rebuild.

"In a fairly short time frame, you hit some of life's largest setbacks: a relationship disappointment and a life-threatening health issue, and these in the midst of the ups and downs that come from running your own business. What were your initial reactions to these shocks?"

"There were low points, more than a few. I had those angry, 'why me?' thoughts. Then, 'What did I do wrong to bring all this on me?"

"But it wasn't that I shut down completely. As I went through cancer treatments, I worked hard to stay attentive to the business, editing proposals while the chemo meds dripped into my arm. It was a time when the tag-team nature of our business partnership helped bridge the gap created by these health challenges."

"You don't appear now, to be living through low points."

"I am not. As for the cancer, I've finished chemo, though neuropathy in my feet remains. But I'm back to playing tennis twice a week and back to a healthy pace at work."

"How did you begin to find a solid place emotionally? When did you see the beginnings of a return to optimism and energy about the future?"

"For me, two ways of thinking helped me get steady. First, it came to me that God might be thinking, 'Delphyne, by going through these challenges, you may touch somebody else.' That desire to help and give has always been a strong part of me, so this view made sense."

"And as for that 'why me?' business, it came to me at some point to ask, 'why not me?' Life knocks everyone around at some point; what matters is what we do to get back up."

"Oh, and forgiveness played a role too, in bouncing back. Deciding to forgive my ex-husband for all the pain made me freer to move on."

"I've lived long enough to have had lots of low points, but I've learned not to dwell in the valley. It's okay to go ahead and have that pity party and be mad and cry, but then I remember I've got work to do. I can't just stay down. So I got on with it."

"At a breast cancer event, a lady I met there told me that people with the 'triple negative' diagnosis I had, that two-thirds of women with this diagnosis see the cancer come back with a vengeance. I thought, 'Two of three?' It scared me, of course. But I choose to not focus on that. I've got to live each day the best I can, helping whoever I can. People are dying every day –plane crashes, car accidents...we can't control every bit of our lives. So I choose not to dwell on the fear. I'm focused on living."

"How has going through these hardships changed you?"

"Let me start with the business. This may not be the most important change, but the fact that it seemed to come from nowhere interested me. When new projects come to us, I used to say, 'Let's take on the hundred thousand dollar project,' or 'we need to win that huge project."

"Now I ask two different questions: the first is, how much time are we going to spend on the project? And what are the profit margins like? The total project may be a hundred thousand dollars, but if the profit margin is only, say, ten thousand dollars, then I'm much quicker to say, 'Hmmm. That's a lot of energy investment to make ten thousand dollars."

"The whole question of energy as a limited resource is a new emphasis for me. That's been a change resulting from the cancer experience that's influenced how I think about business decisions."

"But, I also think I'm more intentional about providing personal support for others because of what I've been through. Recently when my partner's father died unexpectedly, I cancelled a vacation to be with her. She didn't expect it or ask me to, but I know better now the importance of just being there when times aren't easy."

"So with these life changes, how do you see questions of retirement?"

"I'm currently talking with a couple of financial people about that very issue."

"It looks like now I'll need to keep earning income for a while in order to retire comfortably–maybe through my sixties and longer. But that's not bad news, because I like what I do. And I'm finding new opportunities to do more facilitation, which is a special love of mine."

"I have some other dreams, too, of new ventures that will not only help with the income question, but let me create in areas where I want to grow. I'm now working in the area of business travel planning and also playing with a concept that uses my skill in helping people make business connections to the right resources."

"And I'm nearly ready to introduce a women's retreat I've wanted to do for years. I call it Gathering of Sisters. It will focus on developing better self-care; physically, spiritually, and mentally. We will go off to a great hotel for a long weekend; I'm thinking now of a twice-a-year offering."

"How did you come up with the idea?"

"It probably started with some of the questions I was asking myself about keeping strong. A few years ago I did a survey asking women, 'If I put together a retreat for women that centered on taking care of ourselves physically, spiritually, and mentally, would you come?' The positive response was overwhelming, so I knew I was onto something, enough so I reserved the domain name Gathering of Sisters."

"I can imagine three or four days together, maybe starting the first night with a kind of Sisters' Circle, where we'd connect. Then after a good night's sleep, we might spend the next day on a financial focus, like getting our wills, power of attorney, all that in place. Then we'd move on to learning and sharing about other kinds of self-care. My head is spinning with ideas."

"It sounds like you're getting ready to repurpose some of the skills and experience you gained in building your business to help other women. And with the lessons learned through those hardships, you're even better equipped than you were before."

"That's it. I don't see life as an either/or proposition. I have the capacity to continue the business and grow in new ventures too. I think that's part of sharpened ability to focus and prioritize. Plus, the idea of starting a new venture brings me as much energy as it requires."

Takeaways to Consider

- Changes in business, work, family, or health status also change our perspectives and priorities.
- Whether or not you need to continue to earn, choices can be plentiful about the purpose and mode of work involvement.
- Letting go of the non-essential frees you for new possibilities.
- Many people find their satisfaction in helping others to build their skills, connections, and dreams.

Questions to Ask Yourself

- Am I clear about what is really important to me?
- To what degree am I financially prepared for what life may bring or for what I really want?
- How might I recalibrate what I am doing to pursue new interests or income streams?
- What am I hanging onto that I could release and allow for more energy and freedom?

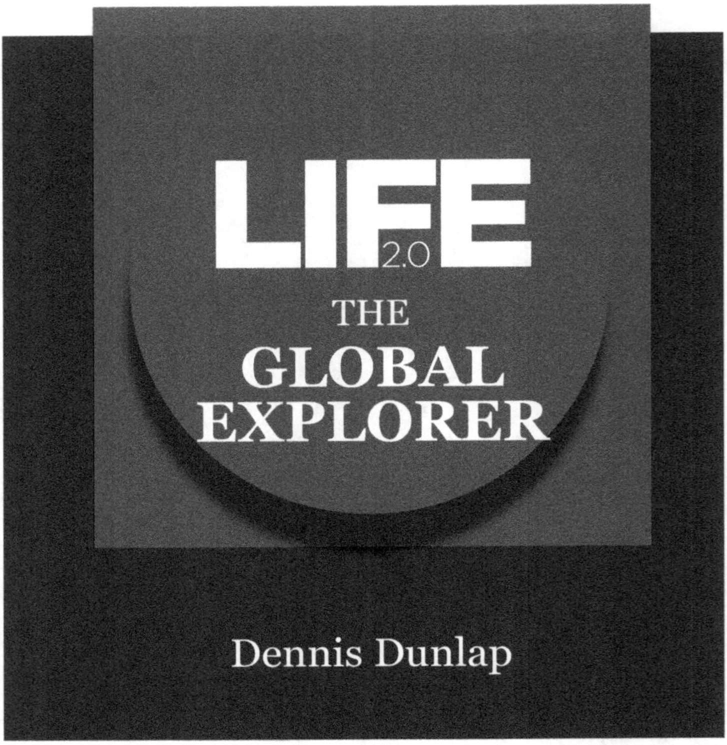

In planning for retirement it is possible to think too small. We may harbor fears that an income drop, or ageism and irrelevance may limit our options.

Not Dennis Dunlap.

At age 72, he was coming up on retirement from his CEO role with the American Marketing Association when I spoke with him. And he sees the future as full of accomplishable options. He's a certified Big Thinker, but a feet-on-the-ground tactical planner, as well.

I think you'll find my conversation with him both inspirational and also instructional.

"So you're exiting the American Marketing Association."

"After 16 years, leading the association during a period of tremendous changes in marketing, I've done what I came here to do. It is a stronger organization today than when I arrived. But, it's time for a different point of view to take them to a new level, and I'm ready to do something else. My successor started last October and the transition feels done."

"Your successor came on board nine months before your exit? That's a long-term setup for change."

"It was actually longer than that. We began the work of succession planning 18 months before my planned departure, defining the qualities in a good leadership fit, setting up a board search committee, and initiating a global search with an executive search firm."

"So you've had a good long time to think about your retirement."

"Actually, I was busy full time with the transition, contributing to a new strategic plan and focusing on expanding the association internationally. I wanted to be sure that piece in particular was solidly in place. So I didn't give retirement much thought until a couple of months before my exit.

"My first thoughts were like most people who've had a pretty challenging and fulfilling work life. That I would finally enjoy our place in Florida, make plans to travel, take up tennis again..."

"But as my final day drew closer, I began to realize I'm just not ready to leave the business world entirely. That I want to stay engaged in business in some way, albeit with more flexibility; to continue working with interesting people, keeping my mind active and adding value to organizations. That's what work has always offered me."

"And honestly, my hobby is work. I do collect art and I like antiques and politics and sports and travel, but I don't consider any of these interests heavy-duty enough to keep me fully active or satisfied intellectually. No, my work is work and my hobby is work. I guess that comes from the privilege of a career that fits and that you really enjoy."

"What did your wife say?"

"She said her big fear with my retirement is that I will be around so much I will interrupt her schedule. She worries that I'm going to get in her way."

"Actually, these comments are her way of letting me know she supports me continuing to do other things. She has a pretty full life herself."

"You might be surprised at how often I've heard from leaders like you that they're not ready to give their days to doing nothing. It's not so much workaholism – a 'have to' thing, as much as it is the joy of activity that simply fits."

"I guess that's me. One thing I am certain about. A company isn't going to hire a 72-year-old guy regardless of how stellar my track record. And I am equally certain I don't want to go to work full time for someone else anyway."

"So what are you considering?"

"Maybe right now it's more what I'm not considering. Though people suggest I'd be able to go into consulting, I'm ruling out doing that as a sole proprietor business. In my observation, to succeed in building a consulting business you've got to invest in becoming a widely recognized expert in some business specialty. That means investing as much or more time in marketing myself as I would in actually doing work. I've thought of teaching, too, and there may be a forum for that. But I don't have a PhD, the pay isn't great, and at this point, doing a good job would require a lot of time in preparation. Though this may interest me later, it doesn't right now."

"It sounds like eliminating what you don't want is helping to narrow options."

"It is. I'm focused now though on identifying areas of interest and opportunity where I can contribute to organizations by leveraging my core skills, relationships and experience in senior leadership positions across a range of businesses and conditions, primarily in professional services. Over the years, I have been involved with for profit and not for profit organizations; small, entrepreneurial, large entities; growth and turnaround businesses; domestic and international operations. And have skills and experience in managing change and transformation, strategic and financial planning, international business, business development and marketing best practices. I also am good at driving implementation strategies and major initiatives."

"Those skills would be highly useful if you were willing to commit to one company or organization full-time, but that's not in your plan."

"You see the issue. And ageism is another potential issue. In terms of mental faculties, I still feel like a young man. But it's the perception of age limitations that would limit options if I wanted to be a long-term CEO of another organization."

"We've talked about what you don't want. What ideas are you planning for when you think about what you do want?"

"I've identified several things on the Want List: I'd like to help companies in shorter-term engagements to grow their business, and I'd like to be paid for my contributions. It isn't so much that I have to work for financial reasons, but at the same time, I want to be compensated for my knowledge and effort. I also would like to serve on a couple of boards or advisory groups at for profit or not for profit organizations where my expertise and experience would be a good fit."

"I'm also attracted to the idea of speaking engagements. Putting together a talk on a research based marketing-related topic that would have high-demand interest in the marketplace. I think I could find a subject that I could leverage in North America and international markets. I have business connections in Asia in particular, so I can imagine speaking in Hong Kong, Shanghai, and Singapore."

"Some fairly different and interesting directions. You're the first leader I've spoken with who is thinking about international options. What's your interest in Asian countries?"

"It's a high growth region so a lot of companies are trying to be successful in developing business in Asia because of the potential. And in China, growth has been driven largely through exports and internal asset structure. But to continue growing at the pace they have been and improving the Chinese standard of living, the country must increase domestic demand for goods/services. Marketing is going to be critical to this challenge. And Chinese marketers must improve their marketing knowledge and skills to create greater internal consumption and to be competitive at a global level."

"You're thinking broadly about the future. But it's easy to see how some of these options could combine your past experience with your intention to travel and keep growing."

"You're right. But whatever I look at comes back to this: what exactly do I have to offer certain organizations that are going to be of value and fulfilling for me?"

"I've been working on a more precise approach and action plan. Do you want to see it when I'm a little farther along?"

"I do."

Flash forward another month. When I opened email one morning, I found a message from Dennis.

Hi Susan:

I have been busy better identifying areas of interest and connecting with people over the last couple weeks.

I am forwarding a brief two-page document ("Opportunity Roadmap") which I pulled together primarily for my own use and sanity. It outlines the targets and opportunity areas of interest that I am pursuing or will be pursuing - although not all at once. Even with a more sequential exploration, it may be too much. I am sharing it with you as I thought it might be useful to see all areas of interest and, of course, welcome your thoughts. Best Regards, Dennis

In the month or so since we first talked, this consummate planner had made major progress in putting feet to the ideas he'd suggested.

He'd decided to concentrate on opportunities with professional services organizations focusing on large associations, non-profits and middle tier companies and providing consulting, placement and search.

He'd narrowed options for making himself known to boards and advisory groups that interested him. He'd identified organizations to target as he explored being an external marketing expert and consulting resource for established firms. He also was pursuing organizations that provided executive coaching and placement for short-term engagements.

But most interesting to me – and most developed in his exploration plan – were the two areas that had obviously been consuming much of his headspace. One area was titled "China Business Endeavor" and the other "International Speaking Engagements."

His considerations for China included some carefully defined marketing initiatives around consulting, education and training, and the development of marketing-oriented events in collaboration with partners there.

As I reviewed the ways he would approach each option -how he'd get information and consider potential alliances -I was impressed. He'd chosen to focus on the discipline he knew best, and was best known for: marketing. Then he had obviously been thinking about ways to leverage relationships in the marketing community he'd built over the past couple of decades.

Takeaways to Consider

- You can still be visionary, thinking as big as you want.
- Both your experience and natural gifts can feed into your value proposition.
- Choose to set aside the issue of ageism.
- Develop your own roadmap with objectives, opportunities, and options.

Questions to Ask Yourself

- What opportunities might there be for me to share leadership skills with other populations, in other countries or in unfamiliar markets?
- What boards, advisory roles, or coaching situations fit my interests and talents?
- Are there ways I allow age to interfere with developing my interests?
- Do I have enough information to develop my own roadmap? If not, how will I go about gathering what I need?

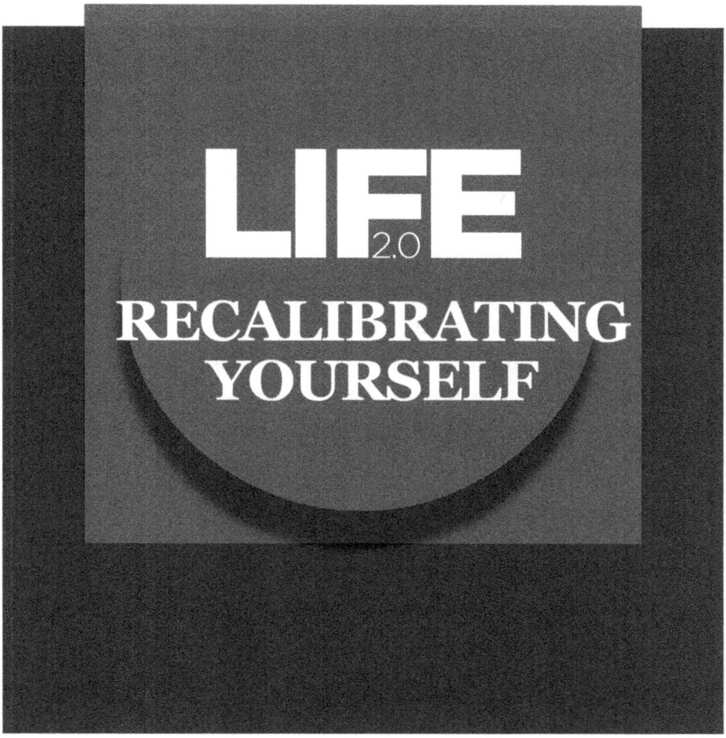

The senior leaders you've met in these pages have all been at work writing their version of Life 2.0. Some adjust their major career focus to accommodate their desire for more flexibility. Others started new businesses. Still others refocused to the not-for-profit sector, and to volunteer positions that utilize old passions and help grow new ones.

The time, energy, knowledge and skills we bring to this moment of life are rife with options. We can generate new ways to do old tasks or throw those tasks out entirely and begin again. The world of opportunity is ours.

But how to begin? Stephen Covey of Seven Habits fame would chide us to "start with the end in mind." And maybe for you, the end of your current career needs some attention before you are free to think about what next.

Checking Your Exit Strategy

I've worked with a number of people who are considering an exit, either from a corporate position or from ownership of their own businesses. I've found these five key questions quickly identifies a person's state of readiness for Life 2.0:

- What are 3 things that are dominating your thinking about your transition?
- Do you have a transition strategy?
- Do you have a transition timeline?
- How have you envisioned your transition?
- How long have you been thinking seriously about your exit from the organization?

You may find that simply answering these questions will provide an excellent reason to start transition planning.

Once you've clarified your transition strategy, a simple three-step plan will get you started. You will assess, then plan, and then experiment to test what you learned.

Assessing with an Inventory

The observations and questions at the end of each recalibration approach were meant to get you thinking, push you to ask questions of yourself. Indeed, part of the strategy behind capturing each approach with a one- or two-word label was to give you an easy way to find approaches that are you. As you read, you likely said, "Gosh, I like the way this woman is going about her search." Or maybe, "I'd never approach that situation the way he did." Either way, in finding what approaches do and don't resonate helps to narrow the field of options. Sometimes knowing what isn't a fit is as powerful as knowing what is. So, with any luck, your colleagues who generously shared their own journeys helped you see better where your story might begin.

With that richness of self-reflection now at the ready, I'd like you to consider more focused questions.

These questions constitute a capture of You, Current State.

1. **The Facts:**
- What are your assets, in terms of skills and expertise?
- What makes you an authority in your area of expertise?
- What have you done or achieved so far to earn that status?

2. **The Positives:**
- What is positive about where you have been?
- What is positive about where you are going?
- What is positive about who you are?

3. **The Feelings:**
- How do you feel right now?
- How do you feel when you are at your best?
- How do you want to feel?
- What is your passion?

4. **The Possibilities:**
- What are some possibilities for what you do next?
- What do you want to accomplish in the near term?
- What do you want to discover or learn?

5. **The Downsides:**
- What might be the barriers or bottlenecks?
- What is holding you back?

The insights you've captured in the answers to the Asset Inventory questions will lead you directly to the next powerful step: Building a story and a plan.

Building a Story and a Plan

There are 3 important elements to your story, which you can directly draw from the inventory you have just completed:

- Purpose - what you do
- Passion - why you do what you do
- Personality - how you want people to experience who you are and what you do

This is constructive no matter the path you intend to pursue.

- It helps you focus on what's important
- Be confident in decision-making
- Engage in thoughtful conversations

By drafting your story you are well on your way to creating your "brand" promise. So, now it is time to design your plan of action. You can be short, sweet and smart about developing your plan by answering these 5 questions:

1. What do you intend to do?
2. What is the point of doing this?
3. How will you measure your success?
4. What resources will you need to do what you want to do?
5. When will you have completed what you want to do?

Now that you have a direction in mind, it is time to put it to the test.

Exploring and Recalibrating

When I speak about exploring, I'm actually asking this question: what small-scale experiments can you try to pre-test your ideas and interests?

For most of us who've led large-scale enterprises for a long time, the idea of exploring through experimentation–especially small-scale experimentation–simply may not compute.

We've spent more years than we'd like to count in group settings surrounded by flip charts and sticky notes, drafting Five-Year Strategies and Long-Range Plans. And as we leave these planning orgies, we're considered successful if we've shaped large-scale frameworks robust enough and set-in-stone enough to contain many smaller plans. Once a company or division plan has been decided, product designs can go forward, ad campaigns can be created and all the rest. Many other decisions down the line depend on the capacity for longevity in these plans we craft.

So, now we're looking at planning that may have major implications for a future under the pressure of a limited time frame, and we're now to think short-range, and dabble in experimentation? Talk about counterintuitive!

But as you plan for a re-engineered future, you'll find this capacity to think Big Picture and plan long-range will work to your disadvantage. It's by far more efficient to think of yourself in the mode of a start-up using the LEAN model. Tell yourself that "small is the new big" and come up with a mini-experiment or two that will let you apply your newly honed knowledge about yourself to see how close your personal insights are to reality.

For example, if you think you have a passion for long-distance hiking, you might plan to start with the 2,000-mile Appalachian Trail, the longest hiking-only footpath in the world. Instead, I'd suggest you experiment. Try a two to three-day hike/camping jaunt close to home. Did you enjoy it? What worked and what didn't? Does it whet your appetite to try more? If so, what did you learn from your trial run that informs how to prepare for the main event?

This "small experiments" approach has become a mainstay in my business planning life. For instance, when I started my consulting company, Recalibrate Strategies, I had some decisions to make about my own market focus. Should I concentrate energy on mid to large companies as I had in the past, or move toward an emphasis on small companies?

Answers to a business strategy question like this could be found in extensive research. However, I tried another approach, a relatively small experiment. I found a company that specialized in small business marketing services and went through their relatively easy and inexpensive process of becoming licensed as a consultant through them. This initiative gave a quick and simple entrée into resources for small businesses and a way to "test the waters" of small business consulting without committing my company to this branding for its duration.

In a relatively short time I found working with smaller-sized companies wasn't the best fit for my interests or experience. Because of the small-scale experiment, I could make a thoughtful choice with experiential data rather than second guessing.

In another instance, I wanted to continue my interest in broadening and deepening my theoretical business knowledge. Some would have gone for additional advanced degrees, returning to the university classroom–a costly choice in both money and time. But to test the idea, I found instead a source for free online business courses offered by top-rated universities from around the world. And I did learn a considerable amount from the courses I took. However, I also learned that giving time to this while developing my business wasn't a reasonable decision.

With the small-scale experiment approach, I was able to see clearly that other priorities ranked higher in my thinking than did formal education. And the lesson was learned without the commitments inherent in enrolling in an advanced degree program.

Exploring and experimenting can work in these ways for you. And as you consider how to invest yourself for the next phase of your journey, experiments let you refine the insights you gained during a personal inventory. Then you can use experiments to refine the action plans you generated from that inventory.

In other words, you can use exploring and experimenting to recalibrate your pathway to the changes you are seeking.

A Model for Life 2.0, and 2.1, and 2.2...

One of the challenges of planning for this next stage of life is our lack of role models to follow. Few who went before us had the privileges we do of longevity, good health and resources to consider new ventures and options. So, mentors to whom we can apprentice ourselves are in short supply.

That's the reason I'd like you to meet my mentor, Polly Swafford. Nearing 90, Polly has just closed down her house and moved to an independent living apartment in a retirement community. But if you speak with her about this change, she'll likely complain a little about the inconvenience of no longer having a backyard for her little dog or the adjustment of now sharing daily life with what she calls "older folks" whose worlds are not as wide as hers.

But what you won't hear are the sounds of despair because for Polly, recalibrating has been a life theme.

As a young mother with two small children, her marriage dissolved in a day when divorce was fairly uncommon. But instead of dissolving herself, she stepped up, dusted off a college degree that had been put aside while she started a family, moved to a new city and became certified as a secondary school teacher.

She jumped into a teaching career, but then during summers returned to school to work toward a Master's Degree in history and education.

As parenting responsibilities became less pressing, her teaching career began to blossom, and she was awarded a Fulbright Scholarship to spend a summer in Brazil. Later, she won a fellowship to study in Japan.

She married a phenomenally creative attorney and serial inventor and entrepreneur. Though he would succeed dramatically, there were also failures-they persevered and bounced back–together.

As her years in teaching came to a close, they together started a local literary publication which would in the next fifteen years become a monthly magazine sold in all fifty states and 27 foreign countries.

In her seventies, one might have suggested her contribution had been adequately rich and it was time for a rest. Polly couldn't imagine such a prospect. Someone suggested she volunteer in a retail outlet that sells Fair Trade handmade gifts and products from artisans in developing countries. This experience became one of ten or more volunteer positions. She edits and publishes a newsletter for retired teachers to stay in touch with fellow educators. And she's served on the board of the League of Women Voters and continues to write a regular column for their newsletter. She volunteers for the environmental recycling committees in her city and for her church and belongs to the Sierra Club. She is active in her local PEO (Promotes Educational Opportunities for women) chapter which helps older students who want a second chance at education.

She helps to prepare and serve meals for the needy at Cross-lines Community Outreach, a local charity and works in their Christmas Store.

Oh, and in her "free time," she pursues her interest in Haiku. Besides trying her hand at writing it, she has attended Haiku workshops and has had her own book of Haiku poetry published.

When I probed for secrets of such a rich experience, the answers came quickly.

"You've described your years of teaching as highly satisfying. Why was that?"

"From teaching and education? I loved it because it never stopped for me. I took on the goal of continuing education throughout my lifetime. I think you are always learning something new, every day."

"And the satisfaction from publishing the literary magazine?"

"Oh, there was joy in reaching out to writers and artists from around the world. It was so delightful to see a submission coming to us from someone in Africa or Europe. Plus, seeing that magazine being accepted and spread world-wide."

"How did you select the volunteer activities you give time to?"

"Well, each appealed to something I enjoyed. For example, I feel very strongly about protecting our environment, so I do a lot with environmental groups. Of course, I'm very interested in politics and government, so that's why I like the League of Women Voters. And at the retail store, it made me happy to go there because it's a Fair Trade Organization helping people around the world to make a living for themselves and their families."

"So, what's ahead?"

"I'd like to get more involved with Sierra Club. I'm not as active as I'd like in light of how much they do to protect the environment. And I'd like to go back to Europe and see more of that part of the world. Oh, and I'd like to hold onto enthusiasm for life. I love that about young people, and I always want that to be part of who I am."

This is the picture of 90 going on 20, a woman continually at the business of generating life.

Becoming the Model

One of my intentions for these years of creating my own Life 2.0 is to offer the world one more Polly, one more person to whom others can look to as a creative source for a continually expanding life.

Actually, what other option is open to me? You see, Polly Swafford is my mother.

This Baby Boomer cohort of which we're a part has the potential to create all kinds of wonderful models. We have what it takes. May we keep ourselves–and each other–assessing, learning, exploring and contributing in ways that make life as rich as it was intended to be.

ABOUT SUSAN SPAULDING

Susan Spaulding is an award-winning businesswoman, consultant, and published author who knew that she—like many others—wasn't content with the "r-word": retirement.

Over thirty-plus years, her work helped shape successful brands for companies around the world. But when facing retirement, she learned to apply her ability to help companies recalibrate their brand to her own career. The more she talked with others in the same position, the more she learned that many of those exiting the workforce weren't ready to retire, nor do they want to—but they didn't know what's next.

Finding out the "what" in the "what's next" was the spark that ignited Susan Spaulding's work in Recalibrate for Life 2.0. As a Boomer with a successful career in marketing research, she was used to finding answers to tough questions about human behavior. Based on the stories of others in search of Life 2.0, Susan utilizes a simple, but powerful set of tools for helping others recalibrate for a deeper sense of self and purpose.

Susan lives in Kansas City. Her sense of adventure has taken her cross-country (preferably in a 1967 Austin Healey 3000) and up in the air (in a Piper Cub) as well as across the world enjoying new places and cultures.

ACKNOWLEDGMENTS

I'd like to thank each of the individuals who participated in the initial Life 2.0 workshop. It showed me the value of sharing stories and providing a platform for framing a plan and what might be a starting place for recalibrating.

In addition, I appreciate each of the individuals who I interviewed for this book. They were kind enough to share their candid perspective of Life 2.0 with me, and with you.

Thanks to those who collaborated with me in helping write, edit and illustrate the stories–Maureen Rank, contributing writer and editor, Kathryn Lorenzen, Executive Coach, Career Coach, and Creativity Coach, Robb Jolly, graphic and layout design and Polly Swafford, editor.

AUTHOR'S NOTE

Dear Reader,

THANK YOU for reading Recalibrate for Life 2.0. I hope you found it useful. If you would be so kind as to take a moment to leave a review on Amazon or else-where, I would be very grateful. Reviews and referrals are vital to an author's success.

I know this can be a bit of a pain, so if you do write a review, please email me at susan@recalibratelife.com and I will forward you my workbook for developing a plan of action as a way to thank you.

Enjoy Life 2.0,

Susan K. Spaulding

Recalibrate Strategies

www.recalibratelife.com

Notes

Notes

www.ingramcontent.com/pod-product-compliance
Lightning Source LLC
LaVergne TN
LVHW021524080426
835509LV00018B/2656
9780997139204